JEWS IN AMERICA

From New Amsterdam to the Yiddish Stage

DE LANDSTREEK

DELANDSTREEK

S. Weck Middelgront

Brams Punt
Krabbe Bosch
Moerassig
Lant
Moerassig
Battery en Wagthuis
Wilden
Moerassig
Cottica Stroom

Cornowini
Mot Creek
Mot Creek

Minie Stroom
Stroom
Cottica Stroom

De Nieuwe Hoop
Tygers Holl
B. Perduin
T. Boeteman

Jan Hard
Jaspers
Woutes
File Monia

't Fort Cottica of Sommelsdyk
B. de Lange Laise
Baas
Gerrit
Bistorius
Bachman
Wamba

't EILANT COTTICA
Stroom

Crais Cr.
Adr. de Haan
Se dan
N. Snelleman
de Graaf
B. Perduin
Makertof
Snelleman
Bricing
le Rouse
Rentshove
I. Leyll
Jan Ridderbach
d'Heer Versterre
Geleyn

d'Alibert de Societeit
Syn Excelensie
't Fort Zeelandia Gouverneurs Huys
Minik

PARIMARIBO of eu MIDDELBURG

Jordan
Adelburg
Belleplase
Bruyning
van Lanken

Claas Moesen
Bruin
Darby
Matthy

Plemper
Commewatranca Creek
Westdorp

Venman
Lea
Vinglon
Volkerfen

Surino Creek
Otto Idens

Weyts
de Weduwe Van Hogenkamp
Isack Mildens
Daniel Mildens
Boogaart

't EILANT SURINO
Surino
Pauwels Creek
Sael
A.link

't Fort Para
Watson
Vreedenburg
Jaspersen
Elsingh
Onfry

Samuel Nassy
't EILANT TUINHUISEN Roo Rak
Banister Creek
Cuevelaar
S. Nassy
B. Jacobs
Clef Nassy
S. Simson
Ian Iacob
A.l Nassy
Mercus
Perduin
Kuichts

De Hr. Secr. Bolle
De Hr. Castillon
Mangelaar
RacaRok
Burgerman
Marie de Britta
Sparjaars Creek
de Fouseca

C. Corbet
Bondeno
Jan Codery
Otto van Vollenhove
Jan Veer
Pieter Jasper
van Schena
Adriaans
Bolle
Wed. de P.

de Heer Vredenburg
Alberty
Ketelaar
la Para
Calison
Jan Vlam
Claas de Camp
Marten Jacobs
I. va.

Cramemeca Creek
Cassewineca Creek
Aron de Silva

de Stat Torarica
Bodam
St. Brid ges
I. Drag
Nagtegaal
Iovari
ca Draagt

L. Gavel
Capt. Taren

Denton

Duvelaar
Drago
David
de Pina
d'Ariab
Don Pedro
Aron
Serfatyn
Munnik
Nunes da Costa
Gristen
Scherpen huisen
de Heer Baffelier
Parada
Barug de Costa

Ioods Dorp en Sinagoge
Nassy
Nansa
Elias Ely
de Silva
Abram de Pina

Curewassebo Creek
Moris van Hagen
Mogge
Jan de Bakker
Jacob de Keifer
Borgerm. Graaf
Borgermeester Manik
L. Holms

Hollant
Montesinus
Schot
Peirson
Isaque Pereira
Nunes
Rafael Aboase
De Casseres
Iosse en Iacob Nassy
Mose I de Pina
Parera
Mesa
Lambert
Iosef Nassy
Solis
Randor
Daegt
Lichtenberg
Bodloo
Wil
Massy
Muinks

Corapinas Creek
Jan Horton

STREEK

LAN SURI

Curbet
Benjamin da Costa
Wilden
Sarana
Jaques da Costa
Cassepour Creek
Saruna Creek
Charle Boket

COM

JEWS IN AMERICA
From New Amsterdam to the Yiddish Stage

Stephen D. Corrsin, Amanda Seigel, Kenneth Benson

Preface
Anthony W. Marx | President, The New York Public Library

Introduction
Jonathan D. Sarna | Braun Professor of American Jewish History,
Brandeis University

The New York Public Library
in association with D Giles Limited, London

© The New York Public Library, Astor, Lenox and Tilden Foundations, 2012

First published in 2012 by GILES
An imprint of D Giles Limited
4 Crescent Stables, 139 Upper Richmond Road
London
SW15 2TN, U.K.

www.gilesltd.com

www.nypl.org

ISBN 978-1-904832-22-5

Library of Congress Cataloging-in-Publication Data

Corrsin, Stephen D.
 Jews in America: from New Amsterdam to the Yiddish stage /
Stephen D. Corrsin, Amanda Seigel, Kenneth Benson ; preface,
Anthony W. Marx ; introduction, Jonathan D. Sarna.
     p. cm.
 "This volume grew out of the exhibition Jewes in America:
Conquistadors, Knickerbockers, Pilgrims, and the Hope of Israel ...
in The New York Public Library's Sue and Edgar Wachenheim III
Gallery, September 21-November 13, 2004."
 Includes bibliographical references and index.
 ISBN 978-1-904832-22-5 (alk. paper)
 1. Jews--United States--History. 2. Jews--United States--
Emigration and immigration. 3. Jews--United States--Politics and
government. 4. Jews--Cultural assimilation--United States. 5.
United States--History--Civil War, 1861-1865--Jews. 6. Judaism--
United States--History. 7. Jews in public life--United States. 8.
Antisemitism--United States--History. 9. United States--Ethnic
relations. I. Seigel, Amanda. II. Benson, Kenneth C. III. Title.
 E184.35.C695 2012
 973'.04924--dc23

Heidi Singer, Director, Digital and Print Publications,
    The New York Public Library
Mary Christian, Editor
Designed by Anikst Design, London
Copy-edited and proofread by David Rose

Produced by D Giles Limited, London
Printed and bound in China

All measurements are in inches and centimeters

This volume grew out of the exhibition Jewes in America: Conquistadors,
Knickerbockers, Pilgrims, and the Hope of Israel on view in The New York
Public Library's Sue and Edgar Wachenheim III Gallery, September
21–November 13, 2004. Curated by Michael Terry, Dorot Chief
Librarian, Dorot Jewish Division, the exhibition was part of New
York's yearlong celebration of the 350th anniversary of the arrival, in
the fall of 1654, of the first group of Jews in the city (and thus in the
future United States).

Front cover: Montage combining a hand-colored engraving of a
standing Native American figure (see cat. 35) and a view of "New
Amsterdam now New York on the Island of Manhattan" in about
1670, a plate from I. N. Phelps Stokes's The Iconography of Manhattan
Island (see fig. 30).

Back cover: A view of New York's Lower East Side (Essex & Hester
Streets). Postcard published by Brown Brothers, N.Y., postmarked
August 13, 1907.

Frontispiece: Nieuwe kaart van Suriname (detail). Map published in
Amsterdam by J. Ottens, ca. 1715 (see cat. 20).

Contents

לא יסור שבט
מיהוד' ומחוקק וגוי

אלהים בורא כל עולמים
כראראפי עולם"עליון
נבהו שס עוז מכיון
אכיס עוליס על כל רמיס

אל רס תכן שמיס בורת
סנקרדיס עולם הגלגלי
שים עם ירח יורדיס עולי
נטס נס ככני קור שס תפארי

חלק ראשון
מספר

Preface
Past, Present, Future—and the Democratic Ideal

Sail, sail thy best, ship of Democracy,
Of value is thy freight, tis not the Present only,
The Past is also stored in thee.
Walt Whitman

It is a signal pleasure for me to write a few words about *Jews in America: From New Amsterdam to the Yiddish Stage*, the first publication to come directly out of the collections of The New York Public Library since I assumed the presidency of this beloved and essential institution, in July 2011.

This Library is many things. It is a treasure house of world cultures, as well as an incubator of human inspiration and creativity, constantly pushing ahead into new technological and intellectual frontiers. It is a nexus where advanced scholarship and the world of universal education are united. And, perhaps most crucially, in my opinion, it is an ever-evolving beacon of the democratic ideal, helping millions of people learn, explore, and become more active participants in our democracy.

The New York Public Library is a local community with global implications. *Jews in America* handsomely demonstrates the global reach of our vast collections, and the expertise and dedication of our librarians, curators, and other specialists—past, present, and future—who serve our ever-evolving communities. By "future" I mean that the world's great libraries must look ahead fearlessly, even as they collect and conserve man's past, to also serve future generations of students, scholars, writers,

researchers, and a general public that is both incredibly diverse and passionately hungry for knowledge.

As a native New Yorker, born and bred and recently returned to the city, I am keenly interested not only in the city and its citizens, but also in the journeys that have brought all of us here, both literally and figuratively. And what journeys enliven *Jews in America*! Ranging from Spain during the Inquisition to Brazilian sugar plantations, from a Confederate cemetery in Richmond, Virginia, to the fabled Yiddish theaters of New York's Lower East Side, *Jews in America* offers a feast rich in incident and character as it traces the history of the Jewish people and their search for an identity—or rather, identities. Vintage maps, photographs and prints, handwritten manuscripts, postcards, theatrical playbills, sheet music, and the rarest of rare books (the only known copy of the first printing of Columbus's Letter to Santangel, from 1493) illuminate these journeys in compelling detail. Languages include English, Dutch, Spanish, Latin, Portuguese, German, and, of course, Hebrew and Yiddish. Multiculturalists everywhere can find inspiration from the saga unfolded here.

This volume grew out of a 2004 Library exhibition that commemorated the 350th anniversary of the arrival, in the fall of 1654, of the first small group of Jews on Manhattan Island, then known as Nieuw Amsterdam. These were the first Jews in the city (and hence in the future United States), a minuscule community that,

cat. 51 (detail)

between the first and second World Wars, would grow to more than two million, close to one in three New Yorkers, including my parents.

That *Jews in America* can tell that dynamic story, albeit only partially, is due to the remarkable holdings of the Library's world-renowned research collections, including those of the Rare Book Division and, here, above all, the Dorot Jewish Division. And great collections are built not only by great curators (again—past, present, and future), but by visionary supporters of the Library, who donate their treasures to the collections and establish endowments toward their growth and preservation. It is therefore a pleasure to acknowledge the Dorot Foundation, whose magnificent 1996 gift, marking the Jewish Division's 100th birthday, brought this historic division both an endowment and a new name; and also the special contributions of philanthropists Jack and Helen Nash, who helped make possible important recent acquisitions by the Dorot Jewish Division, some featured in the original Library exhibition and in this book. And, lastly, we thank Leonard L. Milberg, bibliophile extraordinaire and longtime friend of the Library.

Anthony W. Marx, President
The New York Public Library
March 2012

Introduction

Jews in America: From New Amsterdam to the Yiddish Stage highlights The New York Public Library's remarkable holdings in American Judaica. It also exemplifies new trends in the study of American Jewish history and traces pivotal changes in American Jewish life beginning in the colonial era. Revised from an exhibition produced in 2004 for the 350th anniversary of the American Jewish community, the volume serves as a benchmark, signaling how much has changed since The New York Public Library last commemorated an anniversary of the American Jewish community in 1954.

A look back at the earlier volume, entitled *The People and the Book: The Background of Three Hundred Years of Jewish Life in America* (1954), proves eye-opening. Compiled by Joshua Bloch, then Chief of the Library's Jewish Division, the well-illustrated, beautifully produced album underscored the Jewish contribution to Western civilization and American freedom. It stressed Jews' role in "the advancement of those spiritual and cultural effects and elements which continue to influence the civilized world and which have contributed to the enrichment and benefit of mankind."[1] And it expressed the hope "that from this exhibition there will emerge a definite measure of understanding of the role Jews have played in the advancement of the cultural life of the world and especially of the kind of ethical and spiritual ideas upon which are founded the American principles of freedom and equality."[2]

The focus upon Jewish "contributions" bespoke the manifold insecurities of postwar American Jews. Not-withstanding their status as the largest and most powerful Jewish community in the world, their pride in the establishment of the State of Israel, a welcome decline in domestic anti-Semitism, and a burgeoning movement of Jews from crowded inner cities to tree-lined outer suburbs, they continued to feel vulnerable and nervous. Who could blame them given the unexpected rise of domestic anti-Semitism in America following World War I, the deliberate murder of six million Jews in Europe during World War II, and the fears engendered by the second Red Scare and the conviction and execution in 1953 of Julius and Ethel Rosenberg for conspiracy to commit espionage by passing atomic secrets to the Soviet Union?

The goal, in 1954, was thus to pour oil on troubled waters by reminding readers of Jews' spiritual legacy, the historical role they had played as "People of the Book." Rare Bibles and liturgical texts (found in America but more often than not produced abroad) dominated the volume, which promoted pride in Jewish achievement and labored to elevate the image of the Jew in the eyes of non-Jewish neighbors. In his preface, Louis M. Rabinowitz, the volume's patron, gave voice to the aspirations that underlay the entire project. It would, he hoped, "contribute to the creation of a measure of better understanding of the role Jewish spiritual and cultural values have played in the forging of … American ideas, ideals and aspirations."[3]

Fifty-eight years later, American Jews feel far less vulnerable, and the apologetic strains of the earlier volume have been replaced by bold chords of self-confidence. As a result, *Jews in America* focuses less on historic Jewish "contributions" and more on Jews as historical actors and symbols. It suggests that the presence of Jews has made America different than it might otherwise have been.

The story of "Jews in America" begins at the very moment when Spain's Christopher Columbus discovered the New World, in 1492. That, of course, was also the year that Spain's King Ferdinand and Queen Isabella expelled "all Jews and Jewesses of whatever age they may be" from their "kingdoms and seignories," warning them never to return "as dwellers, nor as travelers, nor in any other manner whatsoever."[4] Once upon a time, Jewish scholars read much into this coincidence, focusing upon the *conversos,* the Jewish converts to Christianity, who funded and accompanied Columbus. Some went so far as to suggest that Columbus himself was Jewish. The American Jewish diplomat Oscar Straus thought that if it could be historically proven that Jews had taken an active part in the discovery of America, "this fact would be an answer for all time to come to antisemitic tendencies in this country."[5] Since the Great Mariner had evolved in the American mind into the embodiment of the national ideal, a symbol of American achievement, progress, and goodness, Jews, in associating themselves with him, hoped to take on these virtues symbolically, yoking together their Americanism and their Judaism, and demonstrating the historical indispensability of Jews to the whole American enterprise.

Today, as this volume demonstrates, most such fantasies have been put to rest. Instead of asking who among Columbus's

circle had Jewish roots, this volume inquires into the involvement of Jews in the Age of Discovery as a whole. Navigational tools, astronomical tables, maps, and accounts of the momentous discoveries all point to the many scholarly and scientific ties that linked Jews and non-Jews across religious lines during that pivotal age. It is not, therefore, the Jewish "contribution" that is centrally important here, but rather the spirit of inquiry that led Jews and Christians to innovate and even cooperate at the dawn of modernity.

Moving on to the New World, *Jews in America* casts its net far more widely than its 1954 predecessor did. While the latter ignored the Jewish experience in Brazil, Suriname, and the Caribbean, in this volume it properly commands an entire chapter. Both Jewish and general historians have increasingly come to recognize the importance of the whole Atlantic World for the history of colonial North America. Scholars today speak of "port Jews" who maintained close ties to one another, sailing in and out of ports, in some cases with astonishing frequency.

In colonial days, more Jews lived in the Caribbean than in all of the North American colonies put together. "Jews found the threshold of liberation" in the Caribbean, historian David Brion Davis once observed.[6] Central features of Jewish modernity—such as the compartmentalization of religious and secular life, an enhanced legal status, widespread social interactions with Christians, burgeoning political involvements, diverse cultural productions, and more varied economic opportunities—emerged in the Caribbean two centuries before they became commonplace in Europe.

The arrival of Jewish refugees from Brazil into Dutch New Amsterdam, in 1654, provides a case study in how Jews obtained legal rights throughout the New World. The colony's governor, Peter Stuyvesant, sought permission from Amsterdam to banish the incoming Jews, fearing that they would "infect and trouble this new colony," and serve as a precedent for admitting other religious minorities, such as Lutherans, Quakers, and Catholics. But the directors of the Dutch West India Company demurred, privileging the company's economic interests over Stuyvesant's religious sensibilities. They ordered the governor to permit Jews to "travel," "trade," "live," and "remain" in New Netherland, "provided the poor among them shall not become a burden to the company or to the community, but be supported by their own nation."[7] After several more petitions, Jews secured the right to trade throughout the colony, serve guard duty, own real estate, and worship in the privacy of their own homes.

For a brief time, Jews held more rights than Quakers did in the colony, but the logic of liberty soon proved contagious. In 1658, the residents of the village of Flushing in present-day Queens resisted Stuyvesant's orders to expel the Quakers, and their famous "Remonstrance" eventually carried the day with the West India Company. As a result, New Amsterdam and, later, New York became ever more religiously heterogeneous. The battles waged by persecuted minority faiths such as Jews and Quakers paved the way for what became one of the most ethnically and religiously diverse communities in the world. Tragically, the only known copy of the Flushing Remonstrance and key

documents concerning the Jewish battle against Peter Stuyvesant were singed or burned completely in a fire at the New York State Library at Albany in 1911. This makes the documents preserved in The New York Public Library's collections especially significant.

In addition to helping secure religious liberty, religious and social outsiders like the Jews also helped to shape America's very identity. In 1954, this theme was explored through the spiritual legacy of the Jews, their special relationship to the Hebrew Scriptures that the Puritans and so many other early Americans revered. In *The Hebrew Republic: Jewish Sources and the Transformation of European Political Thought*, Eric Nelson strengthens this case by highlighting the role played by the Hebrew Bible and traditional Jewish commentaries, which Christians had begun to study, in promoting republican ideals, an egalitarian distribution of property, and tolerance of religious diversity.[8]

The 2004 exhibition from which this book developed went further, however, in pointing to the role of Jews themselves, and not just Jewish ideas, in shaping America's unique identity. It argued, on the opening page of its exhibition guide, that Americans developed something of a preoccupation with Jews—one that reveals less about Jews than about America and the crisis of early modernity:

In the Colonial and Federal periods . . . the presence of Jews in America occupied a sizeable place in the American mind. . . . This is largely attributable to the multiple identity crises of early modernity. The

upheavals of the time—theological, philosophical, political, and
economic—forcefully posed such questions as: Who is a Christian?
What does it mean to be Spanish, Portuguese, Dutch, English, or
American? A consistent by-product of such questions was to heighten
preoccupation with the identity and status of Jews.[9]

To be sure, Jews represented but a tiny minority of America's inhabitants at that time. There were fewer than 2,500 Jews in the American colonies during all of the colonial era, and as late as 1850 only about 22 out of every ten thousand Americans was Jewish. Nevertheless, Americans devoted disproportionate attention to Jews, focusing both on "real" Jews, who settled in the new nation's colonies and cities, and on "imaginary" ones, whom many believed to be the descendants of the Ten Lost Tribes. Between 1743 and 1900, no fewer than 128 different American imprints concerned themselves with prophecies relating to Jews, focusing for the most part on millennial "signs of the times," when Jews might be converted and restored to the Holy Land. John McDonald's *Isaiah's Message to the American Nation* (1814) was a particular favorite. It offered "a remarkable prophecy" based on chapter 18 of Isaiah, "respecting the restoration of the Jews, aided by the American nation, with an universal summons to the Battle of Armageddon, and a description of that solemn scene."[10]

Dozens of other books attempted to prove that the Indians were the Ten Lost Tribes. This theory long predated the arrival of Jews on North American soil. Back in 1567, Johannes Fredericus Lumnius's *De extremo Dei judicio et Indorum vocatione* had pointed to the Hebraic origins of the

Indians as proof that the "final judgment of God" was near. Manasseh ben Israel, the Dutch rabbi who did more than anyone else to promote Jewish settlement in the New World and to underscore its religious significance, agreed. In *The Hope of Israel* (1650), his best-known work, he attempted to prove "that the ten Tribes never returned to the second Temple, that they yet keep the Law of Moses, and our sacred Rites; and at last shall returne into their Land, with the two Tribes, Judah and Benjamin; and shall be governed by one Prince, who is Messiah the Son of David; and without doubt that happy time is near."[11] As did many Christians of his day, Manasseh ben Israel insisted that the Indians found in the New World were descended from Adam and Eve and were survivors of the flood. The alternative—that they descended from a separate act of creation not described in the Bible—was, to him, theologically unpalatable. He also concurred with those who, based on the apocryphal book of 2nd Esras, insisted that the Ten Lost Tribes had scattered to the four corners of the earth, including North and South America. But unlike his Christian counterparts, he insisted that the Lost Tribes would return to the Land of Israel as Jews and remain Jewish. To Manasseh ben Israel, the "discovery" of the Indians as the Ten Lost Tribes pointed to the triumph of Judaism, not Christianity.

As missionaries and inquiring visitors gleaned new information concerning Native Americans, scholars in Europe and America prepared detailed comparisons between Indian languages and the Hebrew language, and between Native American rites, symbols, and customs and

Jewish rites, symbols, and customs. A close look, however, reveals that these inquiries were frequently freighted with religious and ideological undertones. Would the discovery of the tribes serve the cause of Christian theology or Jewish theology? Did the presence of the tribes in America signal that the country was truly God's New Israel? Would conversion of the Indians hasten the millennium? In short, in debating about whether the Indians were the Ten Lost Tribes, Christians and Jews were really debating about deeper issues, such as the veracity of Scriptures, the place of America in the Divine plan, the proximity of the millennium, and the ultimate fate of the Jews.

The fact that Jews in early America concerned themselves with these issues serves as a reminder that, throughout the time period covered in the first five chapters of this book and contrary to what an earlier generation of scholars believed, Jews in America also displayed significant interest in messianic hopes and mystical speculations. Rabbi Manasseh ben Israel, we have seen, argued explicitly that the colonization of Jews in the New World was both a harbinger and an instrument of messianic redemption. No fewer than four synagogues—in Curaçao, Savannah, Philadelphia, and Jamaica—took as their name the Hebrew title of his book, *Mikveh Israel*, thereby echoing the promise of Jeremiah (14:8): "O Hope of [*Mikveh*] Israel, Its deliverer in time of trouble." New York's Shearith Israel based its name on the redemptive prophecy of Micah (2:12): "I will bring together the remnant of [*Shearith*] Israel." The synagogue in Barbados called itself Nidhe Israel based on a similar prophecy of Isaiah (11:12):

"He will hold up a signal to the nations / And assemble the banished of [*Nidhe*] Israel / And gather the dispersed of Judah / From the four corners of the earth." The synagogue in Newport, meanwhile, took as its name Jeshuat Israel, from a Psalmist's prophecy (14:7): "O that the deliverance of [*Yeshuat*] Israel might come from Zion! When the Lord restores the fortunes of His people, Jacob will exult, Israel will rejoice." All alike demonstrated through their unusual names the mystical significance with which Jewish colonists imbued New World Jewish communities, reaffirming the very point that Manasseh ben Israel had made in his book, that the dispersion of Israel's remnant to the four corners of the world heralded the ingathering.

Both Jonathan Edwards, the distinguished Protestant theologian, and Ezra Stiles, pastor of the Second Congregational Church of Newport and later president of Yale College, provide evidence that Jews actually engaged in mystical devotions and practices. Edwards witnessed a Jewish neighbor who immersed himself in devotions and prayers "sometimes whole nights." Stiles watched in amazement as Newport Jews threw open their windows during a violent thunderstorm while they "employed themselves in Singing & repeating Prayers, &c., for Meeting Messias."[12] Stiles also owned and studied a copy of the great Jewish mystical text known as the Zohar, a reminder that mystical Jewish texts and not just biblical ones influenced Americans and formed part of the cultural legacy that Jews bequeathed to the New World. In addition, colonial Jews built several of their synagogues, including the famed synagogue in Newport, to mystically resemble the temple in Jerusalem, complete with its "sacred proportions." They likewise devoted careful attention to the mikveh, the ritual bath. Women no less than men hoped to be primed and purified when that long-awaited, anxiously anticipated event finally happened, and the messiah appeared.

With the dawning of the nineteenth century, Jews in America understood that the messiah had not appeared. Over the decades that followed their millennial fervor greatly diminished. The "long nineteenth century" in American Jewish life, stretching in this volume all the way to the 1920s, was characterized instead by rising cycles of immigration. In 1800, there were approximately 2,500 Jews in the United States; in 1850, 50,000; in 1900, one million; and in 1920, around 3.5 million. Put another way, in 1800, just four out of every ten thousand Americans were Jewish, while in 1920 that number rose to some 330 out of every ten thousand.

Mass migration transformed American Jewish life and reordered the Jewish world as a whole. Over the course of the nineteenth century, Jews spread across the country, taking up residence in every major city and many a town. Where in 1800 the vast majority of Americans had never set eyes on a Jew, a century later they were hard to miss. Jews moved into a wide range of professions during these years, but a clear majority either engaged in commerce or manufactured clothes. Religiously, Judaism, like Protestantism, became increasingly variegated. Large cities boasted numerous competing synagogues that covered a broad spectrum, from Orthodoxy to Reform. Thanks to the establishment of rabbinical seminaries, beginning in 1875, American Judaism also became religiously independent; it no longer needed to import immigrant rabbis to service its synagogues. Culturally too, American Judaism became increasingly independent. Every decade saw more Jewish books produced in the United States, and by the end of the century America was also home to significant Jewish libraries, such as the Jewish Division of The New York Public Library, established as a distinct collection with funding contributed by philanthropist Jacob Schiff in 1897.

By then, New York was the largest Jewish community in the world, far surpassing Warsaw. America had also grown from an outpost Jewish community into one of the world's four largest, the only Jewish community of more than one million outside of Europe. The fact that the *Jewish Encyclopedia* (1901–6), an unprecedented synthesis of all Jewish knowledge, traditional and modern, was produced and published in New York heralded American Jewry's arrival. It proclaimed that Jewish cultural authority was passing to New World shores and that the language of Jewish scholarly discourse was shifting to English.

It took time for American Jewry's new status to be fully recognized and appreciated. As late as 1954, The New York Public Library complained that "not many are sufficiently aware of the presence in this country of a large number of extraordinary Hebrew manuscripts."[13] Today, though, American Jewry stands unrivaled among the Jewish communities of the diaspora. Its wealth of Jewish scholars, writers, and artists; its plethora of Jewish libraries; and its abundance of educational and cultural institutions surpass those of any previous Jewish diaspora center.

The Jewish Division —today, the Dorot Jewish Division—of The New York Public Library has likewise grown and developed, nurturing writers, nourishing readers, and filling shelf after shelf with "books, microforms, manuscripts, newspapers, periodicals, and ephemera from all over the world." In issuing *Jews in America,* the Library proudly assumes its place as a major repository of Judaica Americana, and one of the foremost public collections of Judaica and Hebraica in the world.

Jonathan D. Sarna

Joseph H. & Belle R. Braun Professor of American Jewish History, Brandeis University, and Chief Historian, National Museum of American Jewish History

Notes

1. Joshua Bloch, *The People and the Book: The Background of Three Hundred Years of Jewish Life in America* (New York: The New York Public Library, 1954), 19.

2. Ibid., 20.

3. Ibid., 14.

4. Jane S. Gerber, *The Jews of Spain: A History of the Sephardic Experience* (New York: Free Press, 1992), 287–88.

5. Naomi Wiener Cohen, *A Dual Heritage: The Public Career of Oscar S. Straus* (Philadelphia: Jewish Publication Society of America, 1969), 71.

6. David Brion Davis, "Jews in the Slave Trade," in Jack Salzman and Cornel West, eds., *Struggles in the Promised Land: Toward a History of Black-Jewish Relations in the United States* (New York: Oxford University Press, 1997), 70.

7. Jonathan D. Sarna, *American Judaism: A History* (New Haven: Yale University Press, 2004), 2.

8. Eric Nelson, *The Hebrew Republic: Jewish Sources and the Transformation of European Political Thought* (Cambridge, Mass.: Harvard University Press, 2010).

9. *Jews in America: Conquistadors, Knickerbockers, Pilgrims, and the Hope of Israel: Exhibition Guide* (New York: The New York Public Library, 2004), 1.

10. John McDonald, *A New Translation of Isaiah, Chapter XVIII* (Albany: Printed by E. & E. Hosford, 1814), title page.

11. Manasseh ben Israel, *The Hope of Israel…Translated into English [by Moses Wall], and published by authority* (London: by R. I. for Hannah Allen, 1650), "To the Courteous Reader" [preface], unnumbered.

12. Ezra Stiles, *The Literary Diary of Ezra Stiles, ed. under the authority of the corporation of Yale University by Franklin Bowditch Dexter*, 3 vols. (New York: C. Scribner's Sons, 1901), 1:19.

13. Joshua Bloch, *The People and the Book*, 21.

1

Discovery

The year 1492 was a momentous one in European history, as well as a critical year for Jews and, of course, for America. Events centered on the Iberian peninsula: militantly Christian Spain, united under King Ferdinand II of Aragon and Isabella I of Castile, completed the Reconquista with the conquest of Granada, the last Muslim state in the peninsula. Spain also sponsored the voyage of Christopher Columbus to the West, with the goal of reaching China and India. But a third event in Spain in 1492 was also of great significance. For many thousands of Spanish Jews, this was the year of the Alhambra Decree (or the Edict of Expulsion) that forced their conversion to Roman Catholicism or else face the penalty—in a matter of weeks—of being expelled, in addition to other punishments and humiliations. Through the Middle Ages, the Jews of the Iberian peninsula had been the largest and most prosperous of Jewish communities. In the peninsula, which was divided among Christian and Muslim states, they played many important, albeit subordinate roles on both sides. But from the late fourteenth century, they faced increasing pressure, particularly from the ever more aggressive Christian states. The fifteenth century had already seen coercion, violence, and the decline of the Jewish community on a large scale, and many Jews converted to Christianity. The Holy Office, better known as the Inquisition, was established in Spain in the late fifteenth century and in Portugal some decades later, primarily to monitor the faith and loyalty of these so-called New Christian converts,

or conversos, and to punish those who harbored secret "Judaizing" practices or close ties to Jews, including members of the conversos' families and former communities. While many families assimilated to their new identities, others, including leading Spanish officials and financiers as well as ordinary people, retained an awareness of themselves as something apart. The laws and the Inquisition itself also served to enforce barriers between the New Christians and the old.

Many Jews who did not convert to Christianity enjoyed a few years of security in neighboring Portugal, where forced conversions did not take place until 1497. Other Jews and New Christians dispersed throughout Europe and the Ottoman Empire. The forced conversions and expulsions were significant not only in Jewish or Spanish and Portuguese history, they proved critically important in European history as a whole. In particular, the factors and events influenced the opening of the New World to the European political economy and the creation of the great European-American Atlantic system.

Writers have sometimes exaggerated the role of New Christians and Jews in Columbus's voyage. For example, it is an overstatement to claim that "[t]he epoch-making enterprise of Christopher Columbus was very largely a Jewish, or rather a 'New Christian,' undertaking."[1] There have even been persistent rumors that Columbus was of New Christian descent. But it is certainly true that leading New Christians in Spain, including high officials, were necessarily involved in the great expedition.

For example, when Columbus went to Spain seeking support, he made the acquaintance of Luis de Santangel, chancellor of the royal household, and Gabriel Sanchez, chief treasurer of Aragon, both from New Christian families. They were among those who finally persuaded Ferdinand and Isabella to support Columbus. Santangel and Sanchez, in fact, furnished the money required for fitting out Columbus's ships. It was therefore appropriate that his first reports of the discoveries were addressed to Santangel (cat. 1).

Significant Jewish contributions to the Age of Discovery were in the field of navigation, in developing the tools and techniques that gave navigators the ability to accurately measure the positions of the sun, the moon, and the stars. The astronomer, mathematician, and religious philosopher Levi ben Gershom (1288–1344), known also as RaLBaG, from his Hebrew initials, or to the Christians as Gersonides or Leo de Balneolis, designed an improved instrument to measure angles, which could be used to measure the heights of stars above the horizon. The astronomical work in which this is discussed was soon ordered by Pope Clement VI to be translated into Latin. Commonly known as Jacob's staff or the Jacob staff, this instrument became an essential navigational tool of the Age of Discovery, and it even gets some use today (cat. 2).

Among Gersonides's successors was Abraham ben Samuel Zacuto (b. ca. 1450), astrologer and astronomer to the Kings of Portugal after he left Spain. Zacuto used Levi ben Gershom's work to develop a set of celestial tables that were widely used by sailors. Columbus received a copy of the tables, in Latin, from Joseph Vecinho, Zacuto's translator (cat. 3).

A rare object in The New York Public Library's collections that best symbolizes the entire Age of Discovery is the famous Hunt-Lenox world globe of about 1510 (cat. 4), which is the earliest surviving copper globe depicting the Americas from the period of the great discoveries. Also included are the Polyglot Psalter of 1516, which in a gloss to Psalm 19 presents the first brief biography of Columbus (cat. 5) and the first attempt to describe the New World in a Hebrew book, Farissol's *Igeret Orhot 'olam* (The ways of the world), written in 1524 and first printed in 1586/87 (cat. 6).

Some of the items in this chapter illustrate the Jewish involvement in the discovery of the New World through the development of the navigational sciences. Others are linked to the end of centuries of Jewish life in the Iberian peninsula. While the discovery of the Americas was unquestionably a transformative event in world history, the expulsion or forced conversion of the Jews was one of the most tragic moments in Jewish history. In light of the theme of changes in Jewish identity that informs this collection, one can point to the use of new terms such as New Christians and conversos, applied to the converts (forced or voluntary) to Christianity. Such matters of terminology reflected the reality of the uncertain identity of Jews, as will appear in subsequent chapters.

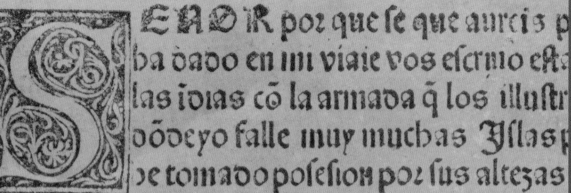

EÑOR por que se que aureis p
ba dado en iiii viaie vos escriuo esta
las ioias cō la armada q̃ los illustr
oõoe yo falle muy muchas Islas
oe tomado posesion por sus altezas
e cōtradicho Ala primera q̃ yofalle puse noubre
tat el qual marauillosamente todo esto anoado
puse nonbre la isla oe santa maria oeconcepcion
ala quita la Isla Yuana e asi a caoa vua non
ui io la costa della al poniente yla falle tan gran
catayo y como no falle asi villas y luguares eul
con la gente oelas q̃ules nopooia bauer fabla
lante por el dicho camino pēsaoo deuo errar grā

cat. 1

Christopher Columbus
(1451–1506)
Letter to Luis de Santangel, Chancellor of Aragon
Barcelona: Pedro Posa, 1493
Page: Opening page of the letter's four pages

Columbus's first word of his discoveries was sent ahead from the Azores, addressed to Luis de Santangel. His detailed and colorful account would serve as a public announcement to all of Europe through various printed editions. His epistolary report brims with genuine marvel at the lushness of the land. He gave Cuba the name *La Isla Juana*, after the Prince of Asturias, son of the King and Queen, and wrote:

[Besides La Isla Juana], all the others are very fertile to an excessive degree, and this one especially. In it there are many harbors on the coast of the sea, incomparable to others which I know in Christendom, and numerous rivers, good and large, which is marvelous. Its lands are lofty and in it there are many sierras and very high mountains, to which the island [of Tenerife?] is not comparable. All are most beautiful, of a thousand shapes, and all accessible and filled with trees of a thousand kinds and tall, and they seem to touch the sky; and I am told that they never lose their foliage, which I can believe, for I saw them as green and beautiful as they are in Spain in May, and some of them were flowering, some with fruit, and some in another condition, according to their quality. And there were singing the nightingale and other little birds of a thousand kinds

in the month of November, there where I went. There are palm trees of six or eight kinds, which are a wonder to behold on account of their beautiful variety. . . . Upcountry there are many mines of metals, and the population is innumerable.

Regarding the native people, he reported on their handsomeness and gentleness and admitted with embarrassment the amounts of gold that they gave in exchange for ordinary trinkets. Columbus appealed to the piety and the cupidity of his important readers in the Spanish court, including King Ferdinand, reporting he had, "so far found no human monstrosities, as many had expected," and that the people of the new lands "all go naked, men and women."[2]

This "letter" went through twelve editions in 1493. The Library owns six of them. Santangel, a wealthy government contractor and powerful advisor to King Ferdinand, financed 70 percent of Columbus's second voyage in October 1493.

cat. 2

Levi ben Gershom (1288–1344)
Jacob's Staff
from Joseph Solomon Delmedigo (1591–1655)
ספר אילם
Sefer elim (The book of Elim)
Amsterdam, 389 [1628 or 1629]
Page: Diagrams of the "Revealer of Profundities"

SENOR por que se que aureis plazer dela grand vitoria que nuestro señor me
ha dado en mi viaie vos escriuo esta por la ql sabreys como enxxeinte dias pase A
las idias cō la armada q̃ los illustrissimos Rey e Reyna nros señores me dieron
dōde yo falle muy muchas Islas pobladas cō gente sin numero : y dellas todas
he tomado posesion por sus altezas con pregon y vādera rreal estendida y non mefue
cōtradicho Ala primera q̃ yofalle puse nonbre sant saluadoz a comemoraciō desu alta mages
tat el qual marauillosamente todo esto andado los idios la llaman guanahaui A la segūda
puse nonbre la isla de santa maria deconcepcion ala tercera ferrandina ala quarta la isla bella
ala quita la Isla Juana e asi a cada vna nonbre nueuo Quando yo llegue ala Juana seg
ui io la costa della al poniente yla falle tan grande q̃ pense que seria tierra firme la prouicia de
catayo y como no falle asi villas y lugares enla costa dela mar saluo pequeñas poblaciones
con lagente delas q̃les nopodia hauer fabla por qu: luego fuian todos: andaua yo a de
lante por el dicho camino pēsādo deno errar grādes Ciudades o villas y al cabo de muchas
leguas visto q̃ no hauia inouaciō i que la costa me leuaua alsetētriō de adōde mi voluntad
era cōtraria porq̃ el ynierno era ya ēcarnado yo tenia proposito de hazer del al austro y tau biē
el viēto medio adelante determine deno aguardar otro tiēpo y bolui atras fasta vn señalado puet
to de adōde ebie dos hōbres por la tierra para saber si hauia Rey o grādes Ciudades ādoui
erō tres iornadas y hallarō iñnitas poblaciōes pequeñas i gēte si numero mas no cosa de reg
imiēto por lo qual sebol uierō yo entēdia harto de otros idios q̃ ia tenia tomados como conti
nuamēte esta tierra era Isla e asi segui la costa della al oriēte ciento i siete leguas fasta dōde fa
zia fin:del qual cabo vi otra Isla al oriēte disticta de esta diez o ocho leguas ala qual luego
puse nonbre la spañola y fui alli y segui la parte del setentriō asi como dela iuana al oriente.
clxxviii grādes leguas por lina recta del oriēte asi como dela iuana la qual y todas las otras
sō fortissimas en demasiado grado y esta enestreno en ella ay muchos puertos enla costa dela
mar si cōparaciō de otros q̃ yo sepa en cristianos y fartos rrios y buenos y grandes q̃ es mara
villa las tierras della sō altas y ē ella muy muchas sierras y mōtañas altissimas si cōparaciō
de la isla de cētre frī todas frmosissimas de mil fechuras y todas ādabiles y llenas de arbofs
de mil maneras i altas i parecen q̃ llegā al cielo i tēgo pordicho q̃ iamas pierdēlafoia segun lo
puede cōphēder q̃ los vi tā verdes i tā hermosos como sō por mayo en spaña i dellos stauā flor
idos dellos cō fruto i dellos enotrotermino segū es su calidad i cātaua el rui señor i otros pa
xaricos demil maneras en el mesdenouiēbre por alli dōde io ādaua ay palmas de seis o de
ocho maneras q̃ es admiracion verlas por la diformidad fermosa dellas mas asicomo los o
tros arboles y frutos e ieruas en ella ay pinares amarauilla eay cānpiñas grādissimas eay mi
eli de muchas maneras de aues y frutas muy diuersas enlas tierras ay muchas minas deme
tales eay gēte istimabile numero La spañola es marauilla la sierras ylas mōtañas y las uegas
ilas cāpiñas y las tierras tan fermosas ygruesas para plātar y sēbrar pacriar ganados deto
das suertes para hedificios de villas e lugares los puertos dela mar aqui no hauria chēcia sin
vista ydelos rios muchos y grandes y buenas aguas los mas dellos quales traē oro ē los arbo
les y frutos e ieruas ay grandes differencias de aquel las dela iuana en esta ay muchas specie
rias y grandes minas de oro y de otros metales. La gente desta isla y detodas las otras q̃ he
fallado y hauido: ni aya hauido noticia andan todos desnudos hōbres y mugeres asi como
sus madres los parē haun que algunas mugeres se cobiā vn solo lugar cō vna foia de yer
na:o vna cosa dealgodō quepa ello fazen ellos no tienen fierro ni azero ni armas nison part
a ello no por que no sea gente bien dispuesta y de fermosa estatura saluo que sō muy temorosos
a marauilla no tienē otras armas saluo las armas delas cañas quando estan cōla simiente
qual ponen al cabo vn palillo agudo eno osan vsar de aq̃llas que muchas vezes me
acaecido embiar atierra dos o tres hombres a alguna villa pa hauer fabla y salir

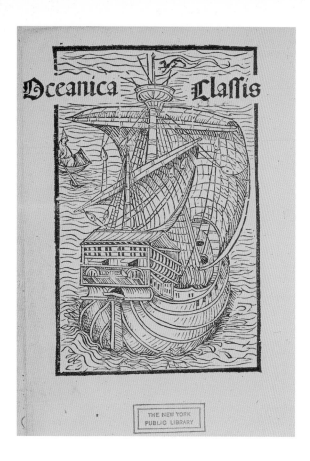

fig. 2
"Oceanica Classis (Oceanic fleet),"
from Christopher Columbus,
De insulis inventis (Concerning the
discovered islands) (Basel: Jacob Wolff,
1493)

This navigational instrument is described by
Gersonides (the latinized form of Levi ben Gershom's
name) in his *Milhamot ha-Shem* (Wars of the Lord), a
fourteenth-century masterpiece of religious
philosophy and science, first printed in 1560. The New
York Public Library has a copy of the first printed
edition, but unfortunately the astronomical section,
with the description of the Jacob's Staff, did not appear
in it. Of his invention, Gersonides states: "[W]e can use
this instrument for accurate observations of the altitude
of the Sun, Moon, or any star that is seen on the
meridian, and this is very useful for our subsequent
investigations. We call this instrument The Revealer of
Profundities for with it many profundities in this
science can be verified, with the help of God." In order to
bring it to the attention of scholars, Gersonides wrote
two poems about the instrument:

*So that man might acquire benefit, God granted him
    intelligence, with it man beholds His pleasantness and may
    visit His temple.*
*Every instrument is provided to him to grant him
    understanding, to know every obscurity in the secrets of man
    and his creator.*
*By means of all the stars in the firmament He teaches man His
    secret, He teaches man His way, His distance, and His
    greatness.*
*Man may consult his rod concerning the structure of the heavens
    and the motions in their paths; his staff will inform him.*

The second poem concludes:

*A man who observes the stars of the sky with me [that is, the staff]
    can open the gates of heaven.*
*He will know the pattern of their orbs, and the paths of the Sun
    and the Moon.*
*With me he can measure that which is measurable, [with] my
    right hand span the firmament.*[3]

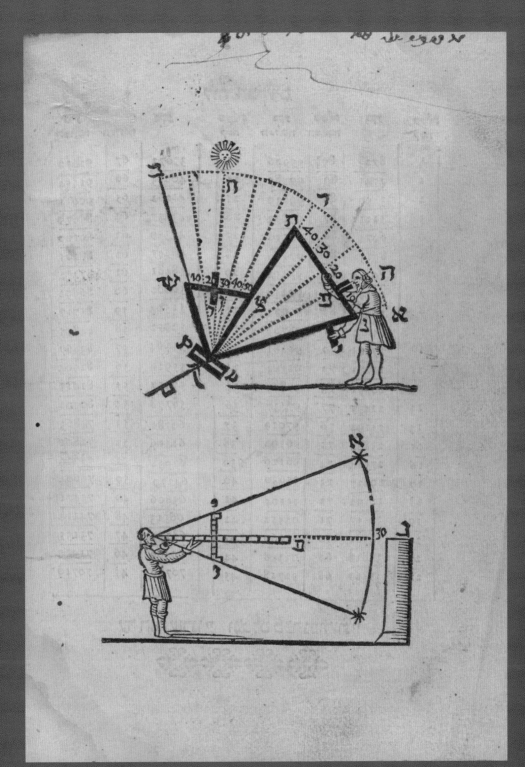

cat. 3

cat. 3

Abraham ben Samuel Zacuto (ca. 1450–ca. 1515)
Almanach perpetuum celestium motuum (Perpetual almanac of celestial motions)
Leiria, Portugal: Abraham d'Ortas, 1496
Page: "Tabula festorum mobilium" (A table of movable feasts)

Zacuto was a well-known mathematician, astronomer, and astrologer born in Salamanca. After leaving Spain he served as the astronomer and astrologer to João II, the king of Portugal. In 1497, with many other Jews, he fled forced conversion, finding eventual refuge in the Ottoman Empire. By the 1470s he had applied modern astronomical technology (such as the Jacob's Staff) to create perpetual astronomical tables, of great aid to navigation; the tables were subsequently translated into Latin. Columbus was personally acquainted with both Zacuto and the translator, Joseph Vecinho, who presented him with a Latin copy. Columbus carried Zacuto's tables on his voyages, and by all reports always found them of great utility. It is reported that this is the first Latin book printed by a Jewish press.[4]

cat. 4

Terrestrial globe, ca. 1510
Copper, engraved, Western Europe

The Hunt-Lenox Globe, made around 1510, is one of the most precious rarities in The New York Public Library's collections. This small globe, about five inches in diameter, is the earliest surviving engraved copper sphere from the period immediately following the discovery of the New World and is among the first cartographic representations of the Americas known to geographers. Of the two continents appearing in the Western hemisphere, only South America is actually represented, appearing as a large island with the regional names *Mundus Novus* (the

cat. 4

New World), *Terra Sanctae Crucis* (the Land of the Holy Cross), and *Terra de Brazil* (the Land of Brazil). North America is represented as a group of scattered islands. The globe is named for the architect Richard Morris Hunt and for the collector and bibliophile James Lenox, whose library formed one of the foundational collections of The New York Public Library.

The story of Lenox's acquisition of the globe is a charming one, as told by bibliographer Henry Stevens (1819–1886), who helped Lenox develop his private library:

In 1870, while residing at the "Clarendon" in New York, I dined one evening with Mr. R. M. Hunt, the architect of the Lenox Library. . . . I chanced to notice a small copper globe, a child's plaything, rolling about the floor. On inquiry, I was told that he picked it up in some town in France for a song, and now, as it opened at the equator and was hollow, the children had appropriated it for their own amusement. I saw at once by its outlines that it was probably older than any other globe known. . . . Subsequently I borrowed it for two or three months, [and] studied it . . . and concluded by recommending him, when he and his children had done playing with it, to present it to the Lenox Library. . . . My pains and powder were not thrown away. Not long after Mr. Hunt presented it to the library, and from that time it has been known and styled as the "Hunt-Lenox Globe."[5]

Psalterium, Hebręum, Gręcū,
Arabicū, & Chaldęū, cū tribus
latinis iterp̄tatōſbus & gloſſis.

תהילים עברי יווני ערבי עם
תרגום ושלשה תרגומים
לטין עם פרוש

Ψαλτήριου Ἑβραϊκου ἑλληνικου, ἀρα
βικον, χαλδαϊκον μετα τριῶν ἑρ
μηνευῶν λατινικῶν ἢ γλωσσημάτων.

مزامير عبراني يوناني
عرابي وقصداني بثلث
ترجمة لاطين وتفاسيرهم

ספרא דתהלא יהודא יונאי
ערבא וכשדי עם תלת
מתתרימא מן לטין וגורהון

es diei apponit,& manifestat

rbum & nox noĉti

ninuit & nunciat ſcientiam.

ŝ eſt verbŭ lamentationis,& nŏ ſunt

mones tumultus & non

diuntur voces eorum.In omnem

ram extenſi ſunt effeĉtus eorum,

n fines orbis omnia verba eorum,

i poſuit tabernaculum,

umiationē aŭt ĩ illos.Et ipſe ĩ mane

ŋŋ ſponſus procedēs de thalamo ſuo

lcherrime,& dum diuiditur dies

atur vt gigas,& obſeruat

currendam in fortitudine viam

caſus veſptini. Ab extremitatibus

lorum egreſſus eius,

rum.

D. Et in fines mundi uerba eorum, Saltem tēporibus noſtris qbᴐ mirabili auſu Chriſto phori columbi genuᴢ enſis,alter pene orbis repertus eſt chriſtiaᴢ norumꝗ3cetui aggreᴢ gatus. At uero quoniᴢ am Columbus frequē ter ꝑdicabat ſe a Deo eleĉtum ut per ipſum adimpleretur hec pro phetia.non alienŭ exi ſtimaui uitam ipſius hoc loco inſerere.Igiᴢ tur Chriſtophorus co gnomento columbus patria genuenſis,uiliᴢ bus ortus parentibus, noſtra erate fuit cui ſua induſtria,plus ter rarum & pellagi exᴢ plorauerit paucis mē ſibus,quam pene reliᴢ qui omnes mortales uniuerſis. retro aĉtis ſeculis.Mira res,ĩ3 ta

cat. 5b

cat. 5

Agostino Giustiniani, Bishop of Nebbio (1470–1536), editor

Psalterium, Hebraeum, Graecum, Arabicum, & Chaldaeum (The Psalms in Hebrew, Greek, Arabic, and Chaldean [Aramaic])
Genoa: Impressit Petrus Paulus Porrus in aedibus Nicolai Iustiniani Paul, 1516
Page (left): Psalm 19 (detail), with marginal note "D" reporting the voyage of Columbus
Page (opposite): Title page

This magnificent volume, of which The New York Public Library owns two copies, is known as the first Polyglot Psalter. The Psalms appear in Hebrew, the Vulgate Latin, the Septuagint Greek, Arabic, Aramaic, a Latin paraphrase, and the editor's *scholia*, or gloss. Known from the eight parallel columns as the Psalterium octaplum, this first multilingual Psalter is a great scholarly and typographical achievement. Bishop Agostino Giustiniani, of Nebbio in Corsica, was a profound linguist and friend of Thomas More and Desiderius Erasmus, and personally financed this Psalter. Psalm 19:5 reads: "Their voice carries throughout the earth, their words to the end of the world."[6] Giustiniani's gloss to this Psalm reports the voyages of Columbus "to the ends of the earth" as the fulfillment of biblical prophecy.

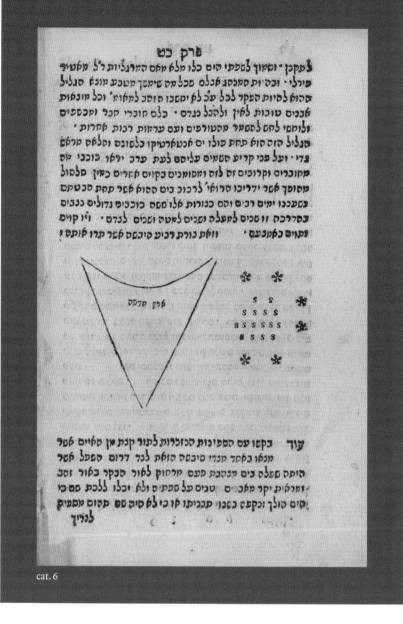

cat. 6

cat. 6

Abraham ben Mordecai Farissol (ca. 1451–ca. 1525)
אגרת ארחות עולם : המלמדת אדם דעת חלקי הז' אקלימים
*Igeret Orhot 'olam: ha-melamedet adam da'at helke ha-7
aklimim* (The ways of the world: which teaches a man an
awareness of all seven climatic zones)
Venice: Zu'an di Garah, 347 [1586 or 1587]
Page: A "map" of the New World, the first printed in a
Hebrew book

This is the first printed edition of the *Igeret Orhot 'olam:
ha-melamedet adam da'at helke ha-7 aklimim*, a
cosmographic and geographic study composed in 1524,
more than sixty years before this volume was printed. It
is the earliest Hebrew work containing a description of
America and is the first attempt in a Hebrew book to
present a map of the New World. Farissol, born in
Avignon, served as cantor in Ferrara. The author speaks
of the newly discovered parts of the world, of the
wonderful stories told by travelers, and of the ten lost
Hebrew tribes who perhaps still survived in these parts.
The *Igeret* was translated into Latin by Thomas Hyde
under the title of *Tractatus itinerum mundi* (Oxford, 1691).
Farissol recounts the Edenic natural beauty of America
that goes back to Columbus's writings: "The land is rich
in natural resources. They have an abundance of fish …
large forests … teeming with large and small beasts of
prey, and serpents as large as beams. The sand along the
shores of the rivers, contain pure gold … precious stones
… and mother of pearl."[7] It also contains the first

attempt in a Hebrew book to present a map of the New
World, though it is no more than a few lines and some
markings.

cat. 7

Biblia en lengua espanola traduzida palabra por palabra dela verdad Hebrayca por muy excelentes letrados vista y examinada por el officio dela Inquisicion (Bible in the Spanish language translated word for word from the true Hebrew with very learned excellence, viewed and examined by the office of the Inquisition)
Ferrara: Duarte Pinel, a costa y despesa de Ieronimo de Vargas, 1553

This is the first Bible printed in Spanish. It was prepared after the expulsions and forced conversions of the Jews of Spain and Portugal, perhaps because the authorities realized it was necessary to preserve the knowledge of scripture and expertise in Hebrew for posterity. The text was drawn from the Ladino version of the *Tanakh* (the Hebrew Torah, books of the prophets, and *khetuvim* or writings). Two editions were printed: one for the general Christian community, dedicated to Ercole II d'Este (1508–1559), duke of Ferrara (hence the usual term for this book, the Ferrara Bible); and the other, dedicated to Dona Gracia Nasi (1510–1569), one of the most important converso women of Renaissance Europe. It was intended for Jewish or converso readers. The translator was the Portuguese converso Duarte Pinel (known to Jews as Abraham ben Salomon Usque); the printer was the Spanish New Christian Jeronimo de Vargas, or Yom-Tob ben Levi Athias.

Notes

1. Cecil Roth, *A History of the Jews: From Earliest Times Through the Six Day War*, rev. ed. (New York: Schocken, 1970), 355.
2. Samuel Eliot Morison, *A New and Fresh Translation of the Letter of Columbus Announcing the Discovery of America* (Madrid: Graficas Yagües, 1959), 8–9, 12, 13. Columbus also notes, "The women appear to me to work harder than the men," a circumstance which perhaps should be seen as universal rather than peculiar to the Americas.
3. Translation from Bernard R. Goldstein, *The Astronomy of Levi ben Gerson (1288–1344): A Critical Edition of Chapters 1–20 with Translation and Commentary* (New York: Springer, 1985), 67, 71.
4. S. M. Iakerson, *Evreiskaia srednevekovaia kniga: kodikologicheskie, paleograficheskie i knigovedcheskie aspekty* (Moskow: Izd. Project Judaica, 2003), 182.
5. Henry Stevens, *Recollections of James Lenox and the Formation of His Library*, rev. ed. Victor Hugo Paltsits (New York: New York Public Library, 1951), 110–11. Lenox's collection was incorporated into The New York Public Library, and the Astor, Lenox and Tilden Foundations form the basis of its collections.
6. Jewish Publication Society, *JPS Hebrew-English Tanakh* (Philadelphia: Jewish Publication Society, 2000), 1431.
7. Translation from Abraham J. Karp, *From the Ends of the Earth: Judaica Treasures of the Library of Congress* (New York: Rizzoli, 1991), 222.

INSULÆ
AMERICANÆ
IN OCEANO SEPTENTRIONALI,
cum Terris adiacentibus.

R.do Spirito
Santo

Ofrus
Marpequano F L O R I D A.
Qalata
Matas de Sal
nalor
R. del Canal
venil
Arenas
Plaia
R. de Flores
Araffo
C. Efcondido
B. de Horros
A Plaia
Tierra llana
C. las baxas
C. Mingualo
Jason luco
S. Maria d' Ochus
P. Chico
Arenas gordas
R. del Spiritu Santo

C. de Gra
C. de Cruz

R. de Montalvos
R. de Ieso

Costa baxa
R. Suelo
Plaia

La Madalena
C. Blanco
Costa d' Arboletas
R. Solo

R. Bravo
Costa
de pescadores
de Palomis
Bartolome

FLO
R. de S. Matheo
B. de Surrunt
R. de S. Augustin
Arbores de
cruz Franseses
R. de los Quiles
Boca de Corrigue
Cabo de Canaveral
Mra. de Canaveral
R. de S. Iuzia
B. de S. Pedro
B. de Ialdena

R. honds
I. del Jardim
R. de S. Iosepho
B. de Tampo

R. de Carlos

GOSFO DE MEXICO

Tortugos

Los Martyres
Cacio

2

New Christians, Conversos, and the Inquisition: The Dutch and the Portuguese in Brazil, Suriname, and the Caribbean

From the last years of the fifteenth century through the seventeenth century, new empires were formed, particularly in the Americas. Spain was one of the greatest and most aggressive conquerors; France and Britain were also leading and lasting powers. But smaller states also set their claims on the new land, particularly the maritime powers of Portugal and the Dutch Republic; both these states, moreover, were defined by their ties to—or enmity against—Spain. This fact proved to be of critical importance not only for the development of the Americas, but for the Jewish involvement as well. Matters of Jewish identity in the early modern period developed in the context of this imperial expansion, and the states and empires involved in it, particularly Spain, Portugal (the sole surviving non-Spanish kingdom in the Iberian peninsula, except from 1580 to 1640, when it fell under the Spanish crown), the Dutch Republic, and, eventually, Britain.

The Low Countries (which included modern Belgium and the Netherlands) had rebelled against Spanish rule in the 1560s, initiating a series of wars of independence that lasted eighty years and left the northern half free as the United Provinces, with Amsterdam as its great city, while the southern half remained under Spanish control. The Netherlands was relatively open to immigrants at a time when religious intolerance marked Europe in general. In the late sixteenth to early seventeenth century it became much easier for New Christians to leave Portugal. Many of

them returned to Judaism when they reached safety. A major Sephardic community was established in Amsterdam; smaller communities were also formed in many other locations. Amsterdam's diversity and immigration allowed the city, a small port in 1585, to become a center of world trade by 1630. The trade and shipping prowess of the Netherlands in the seventeenth century made this the golden age of Dutch wealth, art, and culture.

The Jews were very much involved in the development of the New World, including in the context of the Spanish-Portuguese-Dutch rivalries. In the 1490s, the Jews of Spain and Portugal were expelled or were forced to accept Christianity. While many New Christians and conversos traveled to the Americas from the Netherlands in the seventeenth century, others came directly from Portugal and Spain. Once there, some tried to return to Judaism under the more liberal circumstances of the colonies, notably during the years when the Dutch controlled the Pernambuco region of Brazil.

The Holy Office of the Inquisition was a highly complex organization with a long history and well-worked-out procedures. It was not established in Spain until the late fifteenth century and in Portugal some decades later. Many of the victims of the Spanish and Portuguese inquisitions were New Christians or conversos who were accused of "Judaizing"—secretly following Jewish rituals and practices. After long investigations of accusations by the inquisitors, often

cat. 13 (detail)

including torture, the victims would appear in grand public spectacles. These were important occasions for both church and secular authorities, not least to enlighten the populace and warn them of the consequences of heresy. This event was called the *auto-da-fé* (Portuguese), or *actus fidei* (Latin), the "act of faith." Those condemned to death were *relaxado* or *relajado* ("relaxed"), meaning that the church handed them over to the secular authorities for public execution by burning at the stake (cat. 8). Those who were *reconciliado*—"reconciled" with the church—often had to spend the rest of their days under severe restrictions, up to life in prison. To show that heretics, judaizers, and the like could not escape even by death, their corpses might be dug up and burned in the "act of faith." The Inquisition kept excellent records and published reports of important "acts of faith," such as that of the 1649 celebration in Mexico, included in this chapter (cat. 9).

A significant center of early Jewish settlement was in the short-lived Dutch colonies in the Pernambuco region of northeastern Brazil. The Dutch first seized Brazilian Bahia in 1624–25, but were forced out by the Spanish and Portuguese. Five years later, they seized the Pernambuco region around the towns of Recife and Olinda, north of Bahia (cat. 12). The congregation Kahal Kadosh Tsur Israel was formally established, with rabbis from Amsterdam. At its peak, the community may have numbered about 1,500, perhaps half of the total European population. The Jews played an especially

significant role in the rise of the sugar industry (cat. 13). In the 1640s, the Portuguese in the region rebelled against the Dutch; a long war continued until the Portuguese claimed victory in 1654. To the Jews' surprise, the Portuguese allowed them to depart peacefully along with the Dutch.

Johannes Nieuhof, a Dutch traveler in Brazil in the 1640s, noted: "Among the Free-Inhabitants of *Brasil* that were not in the [Dutch West India] Companies Service, the *Jews* were the most considerable in number, who had transplanted thither from *Holland*. They had a vast Traffick, beyond all the rest, they purchased Sugar-Mills, and built stately Houses in the Receif. They were all Traders, which would have been of great Consequence to the Dutch Brazil, had they kept themselves within the due Bounds of Traffick" (cat. 11). Nieuhof added, with regard to the Portuguese rebellion, "The *Jews* were above all the rest in desperate Condition, and therefore resolved rather to Die with Sword in Hand, than be Burnt alive, which is their Doom in *Portugal*."[1]

In his massive *History of Brazil* the English poet Robert Southey (1774–1843), wrote of the religious freedom Jews could enjoy in Brazil:

[M]any Portugueze Jews from Holland had taken their abode in a country where they could speak their own language as well as enjoy their own religion. These were excellent subjects; they exercised the characteristic industry of their original nation, secure of enjoying its fruits under a free government. Some of the

Portugueze Brazilians also, gladly throwing off the mask which they had so long been compelled to wear, joined their brethren of the Synagogue. The open joy with which they now celebrated their ceremonies, attracted too much notice; it excited horror in the Catholicks, and even the Dutch themselves, less liberal than their own laws, pretended, that the toleration of Holland did not extend to Brazil; the senate conceded, and perhaps partook of the popular feeling, and hence arose the edict by which the Jews were ordered to perform their rites in private.[2]

After Portugal's victory, the Jews scattered; many, including the rabbis, returned to Amsterdam. Others found new homes in Dutch or English colonies in the Caribbean, or in Suriname on the northern coast of South America (cat. 20). Particularly important island communities arose in Dutch Suriname and Curaçao, and British Jamaica and Barbados. These last illustrate that British identity, or at least the possibility of Jews becoming subjects of the United Kingdom, was to become an important option. This chapter concludes with a selection of items concerning the Jews in Dutch- and British-ruled locales into the first half of the nineteenth century (cat. 21–24). The nature of Jewish identity, particularly of Jews of Spanish and Portuguese ancestry, became ever more varied and complex.

Vestitus pœnitentis qui vocatur Sambenito.

Vestitus relapsi vel impœnitentis comburendi qui vocatur Samarra.

cat. 8a

cat. 8

Philippus van Limborch

(1633–1712)

Historia Inquisitionis (History of the Inquisition)

Amsterdam: H. Wetsteen, 1692

Pages: [368]–369, Costumes worn by penitents (left) and the condemned (right)

Page: 373, A procession to an auto-da-fé

Philippus van Limborch's multivolume history of the Inquisition, which was published also in English editions, became well known for its vivid descriptions of punishments and caused such a sensation that it was banned by the Church. Here are examples of garments worn by "penitents" and the condemned. In a procession to the auto-da-fé, those "reconciled" to the church appear in a tunic with a cross. Those in the tall miters and more elaborate tunics are the condemned. Note the effigies of two of the condemned, carried on poles, with coffins below: their corpses will be burned as part of the ceremony.

Eductio captivorum ad Actum fidei.

cat. 8b

35

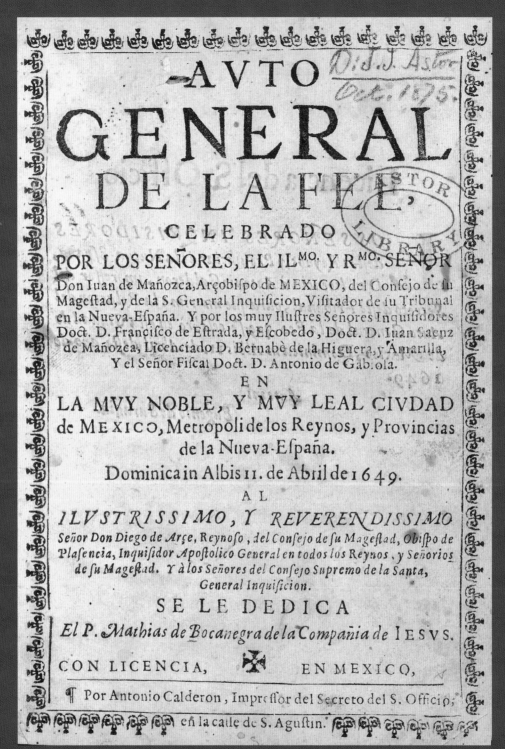

-AVTO

GENERAL

DE LA FEE,

CELEBRADO

POR LOS SEÑORES, EL IL.MO. Y R.MO. SEÑOR

Don Iuan de Mañozca, Arçobispo de MEXICO, del Consejo de su
Magestad, y de la S. General Inquisicion, Visitador de su Tribunal
en la Nueva-España. Y por los muy Ilustres Señores Inquisidores
Doct. D. Francisco de Estrada, y Escobedo, Doct. D. Iuan Saenz
de Mañozca, Licenciado D. Bernabè de la Higuera, y Amarilla,
Y el Señor Fiscal Doct. D. Antonio de Gabiola.

EN

LA MVY NOBLE, Y MVY LEAL CIVDAD

de MEXICO, Metropoli de los Reynos, y Provincias
de la Nueva-España.

Dominica in Albis 11. de Abril de 1649.

AL

ILVSTRISSIMO, Y REVERENDISSIMO

Señor Don Diego de Arçe, Reynoso, del Consejo de su Magestad, Obispo de
Plasencia, Inquisidor Apostolico General en todos los Reynos, y Señorios
de su Magestad. Y à los Señores del Consejo Supremo de la Santa,
General Inquisicion.

SE LE DEDICA

El P. Mathias de Bocanegra de la Compañia de IESVS.

CON LICENCIA, ✠ EN MEXICO,

¶ Por Antonio Calderon, Impressor del Secreto del S. Officio,
en la calle de S. Agustin.

fig. 3
Portrait of Felix Lope de Vega, from
*Retratos de los Españoles ilustres, con
un epítome de sus vidas* (Portraits of
illustrious Spaniards, with a summary
of their lives) (Madrid: De orden
superior; en la Imprenta Real, 1791)

fig. 3

cat. 9

*Auto General de la Fée, Celebrado por los Señores, el Ilmo. y
Rmo. Señor Don Juan de Mañozca, Arçobispo de Mexico… [et
al.] En la Muy Noble, y Muy Leal Ciudad de Mexico…11. de
Abril de 1649* (General auto-da-fé, celebrated by the lords,
the most illustrious and most reverend Señor Don Juan de
Mañozca, archbishop of Mexico … [et al.], in the very noble
and very loyal city of Mexico [Mexico City] … April 11, 1649)
Mexico City: A. Calderon, Impressor del Secreto del S.
Officio, [1649]
Page: Title page

This auto-da-fé, held in Mexico City on April 11, 1649,
was the largest ever held in the New World. It concerned
109 individuals—108 secret or open Jews, plus a French
Protestant who had failed to denounce a friend for
practicing Judaism. About half of the individuals
named, with their crimes described, were already dead;
thirteen living victims were burned at the stake. The
New World wasn't completely safe for Jews, though it
was still safer than Spain or Portugal.

cat. 10

Felix Lope de Vega (1562–1635)
El Brasil Restituido (Brazil restored)
Holograph, Madrid, 1625

An astonishingly prolific playwright and poet of the
Spanish literary Golden Age, Felix Lope de Vega wrote *El*

Brasil Restituido after Spain recovered Bahia, capital of
Portuguese Brazil, from a Dutch occupation force in the
mid-1620s. It was alleged that the Dutch conquest was
aided by a New Christian conspiracy inside the city.
Bernardo, a New Christian in Lope de Vega's play,
describes his treacherous plan: "Having very good
reason to fear that the Holy Office planned to send a
particularly ferocious inquisitorial visitor, those of our
[Jewish] nation living in Brazil who despise
Christianity, in order to avoid arrest, ruin, trial, and
humiliation, have written to Holland inviting them to
make ready a fleet. Things have already grown so bad for
our families that people are beginning to wonder
whether it is true that God has abandoned us. Well, now
we have our answer: the [Dutch] fleet is ready to sail."[3]

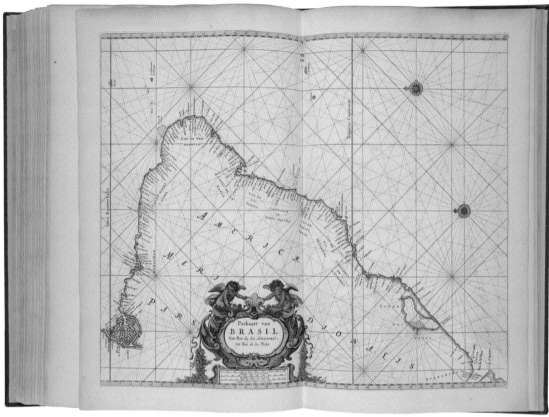

fig. 4

cat. 11

Johannes Nieuhof (1618–1672)

Voyages and Travels, into Brasil, and the East-Indies:
Containing, an Exact Description of the Dutch Brasil, and
Divers Parts of the East-Indies ...

London: A. and J. Churchill, 1704

The neighboring towns of Recife and Olinda enjoyed
brief Dutch rule in the region, from 1630 to 1654; the
province of Pernambuco was the center of the
Portuguese-Dutch struggle for control.

fig. 4
"Paskaart van Brazil van Rio de los
Amazones tot Rio de la Plata (Nautical
chart of Brazil from the Amazon River to
Rio de la Plata)," plate 36 from Pieter Goos
(ca. 1616–1675), *De zee-atlas ofte water-*
wereld (The maritime atlas, or waterworld)
(Amsterdam: P. Goos, 1672)

cat. 12

Caspar van Baerle (1584–1648)

Rerum per octennium in Brasilia et alibi nuper gestarum, sub
Praefectura illustrissimi Comitis I. Mauritii, Nassoviae. etc.
comitis historia (The history of the things that recently
happened in Brazil and elsewhere over a period of eight
years under the governorship of Count J. Maurits of
Nassau, etc.)
Amsterdam: I. Blaeu, 1647
Page: Plate no. 9, "Civitas Olinda" (The city of Olinda)
Page: Plate no. 10, "Olinda"

On the plan of Olinda, the "Excubiae Judaeorum"
(presumably a "Jewish" guardhouse, watchtower, or
other outbuilding) is indicated at B; it stands between
the Biberibi River and the shore.

CIVITAS OLINDA

Fl. Biberibi

Pons

Escholæ
Iudæorum

Hamburgensium
Coenobium

Valli   veteres

Coenobium Iesuitarum

Coenobij

Mons
Rubr.

A. Templa
B. Castellon Lapideum
C. Reductus.

virgæ Mathematicæ

MARE.

cat. 12a

OLINDA

BELGIE

MA

A. Iesuitarum Coenobium.
B. Basilica.
C. Coenobium Franciscanorum.

D. Carmelitarum Coenobium.
E. Iudæorum extulæ.
F. Collapsa urbis mœnia.

G. Castrum maritimum.
H. Statio navium Reciffæ.
I. Reciffa.

K. Mauritiopolis.
L. Promontorium S. Augustini.
M. Oceanus.

cat. 12b

cat. 13

John Ogilby (1600–1676)

America: Being the Latest and Most Accurate Description of the New World…

London: [J. Ogilby], 1671

Page (right): 504, "The Manner of making sugar in the sugar-mills"

Page (opposite): fold-out plate, following page 482, "Mauritiopolis"

Page (overleaf): between pages 304 and 305, "Insulae Americanae"

Prince Johan Maurits (1604–1679) was appointed governor of Dutch possessions in Brazil by the West India Company in 1636, serving till 1644. He added to its territories and transformed Recife by building a new town, which he named after himself—Mauritsstad (in Dutch) or Mauritiopolis—and which is captured in this view from John Ogilby's *America* (1671). Ogilby comprehensively documented the discoveries of the New World, including "their cities, fortresses, towns, temples, mountains, and rivers," the "remarkable voyages thither," and the "several European plantations in those parts." One plate illustrates the workings of a sugar mill; the Jews of the New World played major roles in the development of the sugar industry. *America* is "adorn'd with maps and sculptures [engravings]," including a handsome map of the Caribbean region, "Insulae Americanae in oceano septentrionali, cum terris adiacentibus" (The American islands in the Northern Ocean, with the adjacent lands).

cat. 13a

MAURITIOPOLIS

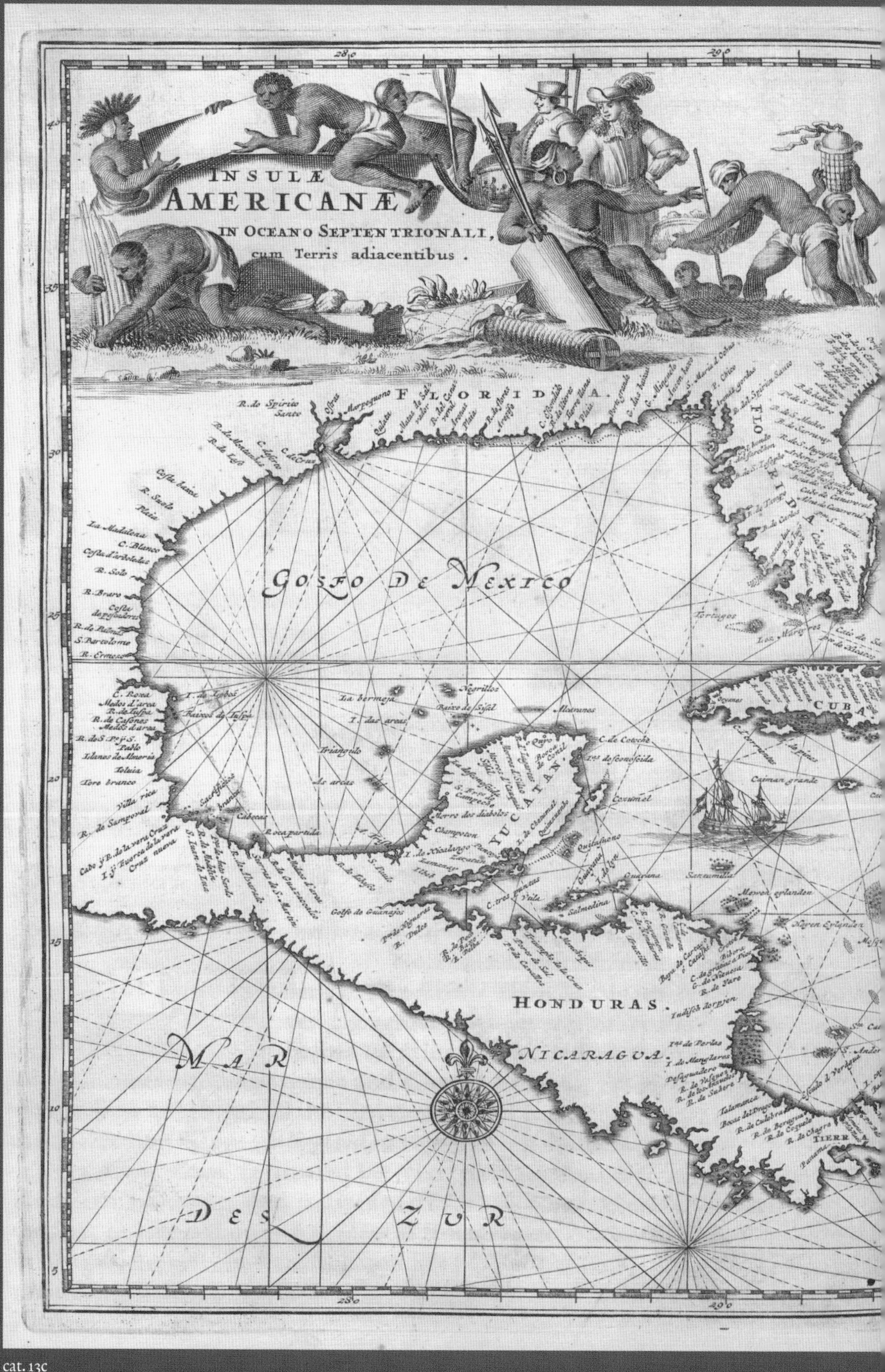

INSULÆ
AMERICANÆ
IN OCEANO SEPTENTRIONALI,
cum Terris adiacentibus.

F L O R I D A.

FLORIDA.

GOLFO DE MEXICO

CUBA

HONDURAS.

NICARAGVA

M A R

D E S Z V R

TIERR

300

320

Barra de S.t F005 oft
van Chesapeac

B. de la Malalena

C. de engano

M A R   D E S

La Bermuda

N O R T

CARTAGENA   S. MARTHA   VENEZUELA

Milliaria Germanica

Milliaria Hispanica

300

320

cat. 14

Hayyim Shabbetai (ca. 1555–1647)

ספר תורת חיים

Sefer Torat Hayim (Responsa of Hayyim Shabbetai)
Salonika: Nidpas al yede ha-madpisim ha-shutafim
Avraham b.k.m. ha-r. David Nahman veha-r: Yom Tov
b.k.r. Mosheh Konfilias, 473–482 [1712 or 1713–22]
Page: 'Olelot ha-kerem [Book page with question or
response]

This collection of rulings on Jewish religious law
includes the New World's first contribution to the vast
body of Jewish responsa literature. The inquiry was sent
by the Recife Jewish community to Hayyim Shabbetai,
Rabbi of Salonika, Greece (then in the Ottoman Empire),
and one of the outstanding scholars of his time. (He was
known from his Hebrew initials as the MaHaRCHa"SH.)

The circumstances of living in a tropical climate
(Recife has an average annual rainfall of seventy
inches)—moreover, with the seasons reversed in the
Southern Hemisphere—led the Brazilian Jews to ask
whether they could change the season for reciting the
prayer for dew and rain (*tal u-matar*, in Hebrew) to a time
more appropriate for their circumstances. The prayers
were traditionally made in the fall and winter—the
rainy season in the Eastern Mediterranean—but as they
explained in their original question, too much winter
rain caused diseases and epidemics. This matter came
up repeatedly as the Jews moved out of their original
homeland and settled in regions with radically different
climates. The decision came down to resolving the
tension between tradition and Jewish unity on the one
hand, and mundane local needs on the other. The
rabbi's answer was that they should not pray for rain
when it could be harmful, but they should not recite the
prayer at a nontraditional time. "Shabbetai obviously
chose a middle path. . . . His only recourse, or so it must
have seemed to him, was to suggest, in effect, that the
Jews of Recife ignore the prayer for rain."[4]

cat. 15

Isaac da Fonseca Aboab (1605–1693)
Parafrasis Comentado sobre el Pentateuco (Paraphrastic
commentary on the Pentateuch)
Amsterdam: Cordova, 1681
Page: Title page

Isaac da Fonseca Aboab, born in Portugal, fled that
country with his parents, eventually reaching
Amsterdam, where he studied under local rabbis. In
1639 he became a *Haham* (literally, "wise man" or "sage,"
a Sephardic rabbi) in Amsterdam's consolidated
Sephardic synagogue. In 1642 he accepted a call as
Haham in Recife, and became the first rabbi to serve in
the Americas. The question about the prayer for rain,
sent to Rabbi Hayyim Shabbethai (see cat. 14), came from
Aboab's Tsur Israel congregation. After the Portuguese

cat. 16   cat. 17

victory in 1654, Aboab returned to Amsterdam with many of the Jews. Aboab, well known as a mystic and kabbalist, was a member of the board that excommunicated Benedict (Baruch) Spinoza in 1656. This Spanish-language translation and commentary on the Hebrew scriptures was prepared to help the New Christians returning to Judaism in the Netherlands.

cat. 16

סליחות לאשמורות הבקר ותחינות ימי התעניות ויום כפור קטן

Selihot le-ashmurot ha-boker u-tehinot yeme ha-taaniyot ve-Yom kipur katan (Penitential prayers for dawn and supplications for the fast-days and the minor Day of Atonement)
Amsterdam: David de Castro Tartas, 5426 AM (1666)
Page: Title page

Aboab (see cat. 15) briefly became a follower of Shabbethai Tzevi (ca. 1626–1676), a self-proclaimed Jewish messiah. For a few months in 1666, Jews in many countries came to believe that the long-awaited messiah had finally appeared in the person of this charismatic kabbalist from Smyrna (now Izmir, Turkey). This belief was short-lived and was generally disavowed after the news came that Shabbethai Tzevi had converted to Islam. The excitement surrounding the sudden rise and fall of the Shabbathaian movement led to fervent calls for repentance and the publication of penitential

prayers, a common response to catastrophe in the Jewish world. The title page of this prayer book uses a messianic allusion embedded in a biblical verse (Zechariah 8:7), while the colophon on the final page states that it was printed in "year one of the messiah."

cat. 17

Saul Levi Mortera (ca. 1596–1660)
Providencia de Dios con Ysrael, Verdad y Eternidad de la Ley de Moseh y Nulidad de las Demas Leias (God's providential care for Israel, the truth and permanence of the Law of Moses, and the nullity of other religions)
Amsterdam, 1689
Page: Title page

This 1689 manuscript is a Spanish translation from the Portuguese original, written in 1659. Mortera (or Morteira), born in Italy, became a rabbi at the Portuguese synagogue in Amsterdam. He wrote the work as a polemic against Dutch Calvinism. It circulated in manuscript only; it finally saw print in 1988. This copy was translated by Moses Raphael d'Aguilar (d. ca. 1679), who served as a rabbi in Brazil in the 1640s, and was subsequently copied by Solomon the Salonikan. In chapter 11 Mortera presented the negotiated surrender of the city of Recife to the Portuguese in 1654 as proof of God's "providential care" for the Jews. That is, instead of allowing the Portuguese to kill the Jews or hand them over to the Inquisition, "God inspired [Portuguese] Governor Barreto to have it proclaimed in the streets that nobody should so much as touch anyone of the Hebrew nation on pain of severe punishment. Not only that, but he allowed them to sell their possessions and provided passage to Holland for all 600 that remained. For want of Dutch ships, he managed to find them Portuguese ones, and so they boarded 16 vessels, many old and rickety—yet, by divine grace and providence, every one of them arrived safely."[5] Rabbi Mortera was also a member of the board that excommunicated Spinoza in 1656.

cat. 18

Manoel Calado (1584–1654)
O valeroso lucideno. E triumpho da liberdade. Primeira parte. Tratase da restauraçam de Parnambuco, & da expulsaõ dos olandeses, do estado do Brasil (The valorous Lusitanian, and the triumph of liberty. First part. Dealing with the restoration of Pernambuco and the expulsion of the Dutch from the state of Brazil)
Lisbon: P. Craesbeeck, impressor, & liureiro das Ordẽs militares, 1648
Page: Title page

Manoel Calado, a Portuguese priest, gives the other side of the story of the struggle for Pernambuco. Only the first part ever appeared in print; the 1648 edition was

suppressed, but relicensed and republished twenty years later (the Library has copies of both editions). Calado stated that many Portuguese New Christians declared themselves to be Jews when the Dutch took over, but others remained Catholic or even reconverted to Catholicism. This example illustrates that the matter of identity among the New Christians and conversos was extraordinarily complicated.

cat. 19

Alexandre Olivier Exquemelin (ca. 1645–1707)
Piratas de la America, y luz a la defensa de las costas de Indias Occidentales (Pirates of America, and elucidation of the coastal defense of the West Indies)
Cologne: Struickman, 1681
Page: Title page

This was a very popular work on pirates from England, France, and elsewhere operating in the Caribbean and South and Central America. The book was translated into several languages shortly after this first edition of the Spanish translation was made from the original Dutch edition of 1678; this was the source of the subsequent English and French translations. The importance of this work for Jewish history lies in the contribution of Miguel (Daniel Levi) de Barrios (1635–1701), a converso poet and chronicler of the Portuguese Jewish community of Amsterdam. He was perhaps its

O
VALEROSO
LVCIDENO,
E
TRIVMPHO
DA
LIBERDADE,
PRIMEIRA PARTE.

COMPOSTA

POR O P. MESTRE FREI MANOEL CALADO
da Ordem de S. Paulo primeiro Ermitão, da Congregação dos
Eremitas da Serra d'Ossa, natural de Villauiçosa.

DEDICADA

AO SERENISSIMO SENHOR DOM THEODOSIO
Principe do Reyno, & Monarchia de Portugal.

EM LISBOA.

Com licença da Sancta Inquisição, Ordinario, & Mesa do Paço.

Por Paulo Craesbeeck, Impressor, & liureiro das Ordēs Militares.
Anno do Senhor de 1648.

cat. 18

PIRATAS
DE LA
AMERICA,
Y luz à la defensa de las costas de
Indias Occidentales.

DEDICADO
A
DON BERNARDINO ANTONIO
De Pardiñas Villar- de Fransos,
Cavallero del Orden de S. Tiago, Secretario del Ex.mo Sr.
Duque de Medina-Cœli, en el empleo de Primer
Ministro de su Magestad Catholica.

POR EL ZELO Y CUYDADO DE
DON ANTONIO FREYRE,
Natural de la Inclyta Ciudad de la Coruña en el Reyno de
Galicia, y Vezino de la Herculeä de Cadiz.

Traducido de la lengua Flamenca en Española, por el
Dor. ALONSO DE BUENA-MAISON,
Español, Medico Practico en la Amplissima y Magnifica
Ciudad de Amsterdam.

Impresso en COLONIA AGRIPPINA, en Casa de
LORENZO STRUICKMAN. Año de 1681.

cat. 19

first professional freelance writer, living by his pen. First, however, he reached the rank of captain in the Spanish army in Flanders, then settled in Holland, living openly as a Jew. He, too, briefly became a follower of Shabbethai Tzevi (see cat. 16). Barrios contributed a long, descriptive poem to *Piratas de la America*, entitled "Descripcion de las Islas del Mar Athlantico y de America" (Description of the islands of the Atlantic Ocean and of America). The poem moves from Spain and the Atlantic islands to the Caribbean, including the islands of Trinidad, Tobago, Puerto Rico, Barbados, Jamaica, and "Hispaniola, called Haiti by the Indians." He had made the voyage to Tobago with his wife in 1660, but she died shortly after their arrival, and he returned to Europe. Barrios's poem is one of the earliest extended works specifically devoted to America by a Jewish writer.

cat. 20

Nieuwe kaart van Suriname
(New map of Suriname)
Amsterdam: J. Ottens, ca. 1715

The origins of the Jewish community in this country on the Caribbean coast of South America can be traced back to the 1630s, first under English and then Dutch rule. Typically the Jews were descendants of conversos whose families had fled the Iberian peninsula. Visible on this detailed map of the northeastern part of the colony (see

also close-up, p. 2) are the names of many of the Jewish landowners whose plantations were located along the Suriname River—note the common Spanish or Portuguese Jewish names, such as de Fonseca, de Pina, Serfatyn, da Costa, Nassy, Elias, da Silva, etc. Also depicted is the "Joods Dorp en Sinagoge" (Jews' town and synagogue). The early Jewish settlement centered on the synagogue would later be called Joden Savanna (Jews' Savannah).

cat. 21

Beschryving van de plechtigheden nevens de lofdichten en gebeden uitgesproken op het eerste jubelfeest van de synagogue der Portugeesche joodsche gemeente, op de savane in der colonie Suriname, genaamd zegen en vrede, op den 12den van Wynmaand des jaars MDCCLXXXV.
(Description of the celebrations as well as the panegyrics and prayers pronounced at the first Jubilee Festival of the synagogue of the Portuguese Jewish congregation, on the savanna in the colony of Suriname, called Blessings and Peace, on the 12th of October of the year 1785)
Amsterdam: Dronsberg, [1786]

In 1785 the Jewish community of Suriname celebrated the centennial of its synagogue. This booklet presents the program for the occasion, including a description of the event, a list of participants, poetry composed for it, and the text of the cantata. The Amsterdam Portuguese synagogue frequently commissioned special works for

cat. 20

important occasions; the synagogue in Suriname would have taken its material from there, though this program does not give the name of the composer.[6]

cat. 22

David de Isaac Cohen Nassy
(1747–1806)
Programma de huma caza d'educacao, ou seminario de criaturas na savanna de judeus (Program of a house of education or seminary for children in the Savanna of the Jews)
Paramaribo: Officina de A. Soulage Junior, a custas des emprendores, 1796

This prospectus published in Paramaribo, the capital of Suriname, in 1796 presented a plan to establish a subsidized boarding school to educate Jewish children. It cites the "immortal [Moses] Mendelssohn," the founder of the Jewish enlightenment in Germany, as inspiration (p. 7). The text of the proposal appears in three languages: Portuguese, French, and Dutch. The author provided what appear to be somewhat garbled references to North American educational establishments in Princeton, New Jersey, and Cambridge, Massachusetts, as successful examples: "in Pensylvania *Bet-lehem, Prinstown*; in Boston, *New Cambridge*" (p. 8).

cat. 23

Low's Pocket Companion, and Complete Annual Leeward Island Register, for MDCCXCIV
Basseterre, St. Christopher's: E. L. Low, 1793

This almanac was intended for use throughout the Leeward Islands. In addition to a variety of typical calendar information, it includes a page devoted to "Jewish festivals, to be observed in the year 1794." Although there was no Jewish community on St. Christopher (St. Kitts), there were thriving Jewish communities in Barbados, Jamaica, Suriname, and elsewhere. Almanacs published in Jamaica included a Jewish calendar as early as 1776. Edward Luther Low, the printer and bookseller who produced this almanac, must have realized that the inclusion of Jewish holidays would increase its usefulness among Jewish merchants in the Caribbean and the Christians who dealt with them. (There are, however, several errors in dates.) The Library's copy of this edition, purchased in 2011, is unique.

cat. 24

Toleration Laws, Jamaica: Copies of the Laws Passed by the Several Colonial Legislatures for the Relief of the Catholics, the Removal of the Disabilities of the Jews, and of Free Persons of Colour, during the Last Six Years (as far as relates to the Island of Jamaica)
London: Ordered by the House of Commons to be printed, 1832

Toleration Laws, West Indies: Copies of the Laws Passed by the Several Colonial Legislatures for the Relief of the Catholics, the Removal of the Disabilities of the Jews, and of Free Persons of Colour, during the Last Six Years
London: Ordered by the House of Commons to be printed, 1832

England had great difficulty granting civil equality to the Jews (and to other minorities); it took place in the colonies before the home country. These Toleration Laws, issued in January and April 1832, respectively, pull together the important acts. In Jamaica, there is the 1827 "Act to entitle Jews, born within the legiance of the King's to the rights and privileges of other natural-born British subjects" and in 1830, "An Act . . . for relief of His Majesty's subjects of the Jewish persuasion." The collection on the West Indies covers Antigua, Barbados, the Bahamas, Dominica, Grenada, St. Christopher, St. Vincent, Tobago, and the Virgin Islands, including Tortola. In the latter islands, the only specific reference to the Jews concerns Barbados, the British island with the most significant Jewish population (after Jamaica), "An Act for the relief of His Majesty's subjects in this island who profess the Jewish religion" (1831). The laws in these booklets brought to a successful close the long struggle for Jewish emancipation in British colonial America, a struggle that continued in Britain itself for another generation.

Notes

1. Johannes Nieuhof, *Voyages and Travels, into Brasil, and the East-Indies: Containing, an Exact Description of the Dutch Brasil, and Divers Parts of the East-Indies* . . . (London: A. and J. Churchill, 1704), 146, 123.

2. Robert Southey, *History of Brazil* (London: Longman, Hurst, Rees, and Orme, 1810–19), 1: 566.

3. Arnold Wiznitzer, *Jews in Colonial Brazil* (New York: Columbia University Press, 1960), 208–9.

4. Arnold A. Lasker and Daniel J. Lasker, "The Jewish Prayer for Rain in the Post-Talmudic Diaspora," *AJS Review* 9, no. 2 (Autumn 1984): 162–64.

5. H. P. Salomon, ed., *Saul Levi Mortera: Tratado da verdade da lei de Moisés: escrito pelo seu próprio punho em Português; edição facsimilada, leitura do autógrafo (1659), introdução e comentário por H. P. Salomon* (Coimbra: Por ordem da Universidade, 1988), 75–76.

6. Personal communications with Cantor Dr. Josee Wolff and Rev. Salomon L. Vas Dias, June 2, 2011.

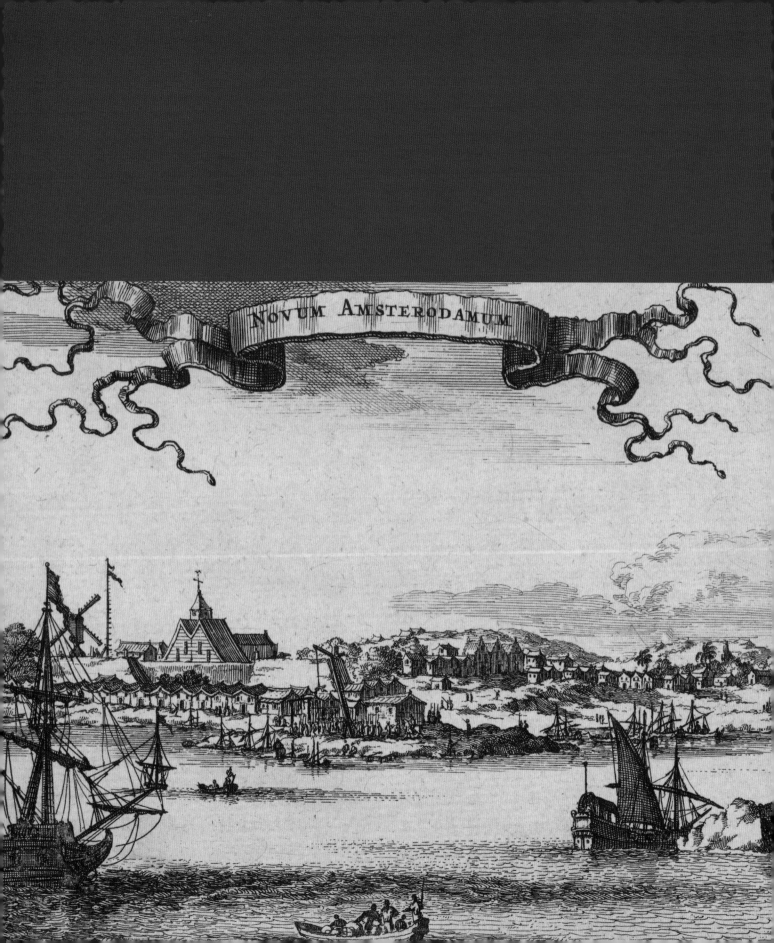

3

Arriving in New Amsterdam—and then, New York

The early and middle decades of the seventeenth century saw a great rush by European states and empires to establish colonies along the eastern coast of North America. The Netherlands' efforts were focused on the islands and mainland around what is now called New York Bay and the Hudson River Estuary; that is, today's New York City, and parts of Long Island, New Jersey, and northward into the Hudson River Valley. The territories were controlled by the Dutch West India Company, which sought desperately to encourage immigration and spur economic growth. The key point for the Company was to earn money for its stockholders. This fact was to play a critical role in the arrival of Jews in the region.

While the records are sparse and often unclear, they first indicate Jews coming to New Amsterdam in the summer of 1654. They included traders who came via Amsterdam or London. The names of three individuals are known; each had passports from the Company. Of particular significance is Asser Levy, the only one who stayed in the colony—until his death in 1682—and who appears over the decades in the documentary record. Levy was of Ashkenazic rather than Sephardic or New Christian descent, coming from Vilna (or Wilno, then a major city of the Polish-Lithuanian Commonwealth, now Vilnius, capital of independent Lithuania).

Another, more popular story of the beginnings of the North American Jewish community refers to a ship arriving in September 1654, bearing twenty-three refugees—men, women, and children—from Portuguese Brazil after the defeat of the Dutch. These were supposed to be the founders of the community. Records do, in fact, show that a ship arrived with a number of impoverished Jews at this time, and that New Amsterdam was troubled with these new arrivals.[1] The director-general of the colony, Peter Stuyvesant, argued that the impoverished Jews should not be allowed to remain; he seems not to have objected to the traders with company passports. In following years, Stuyvesant repeatedly argued against a permanent Jewish presence, both for religious reasons and because of his dislike of Jewish traders competing with Christian traders. The directors of the Dutch West India Company, in their turn, rejected his arguments, stating that the colony needed more people, and moreover that Jews among the company's stockholders had asked that Jews be permitted to live and work in New Amsterdam. This set a pattern for the last years of Dutch rule: Stuyvesant tried to limit the Jewish presence, and the Company, presumably because of the efforts of its stockholders and their connections, preferred to allow the Jewish presence.

In 1664, the English conquered the city and renamed it and the larger province New York, otherwise largely allowing things to continue much as they were. Through the 1660s and '70s evidence of a Jewish presence is sparse. But by the end of the seventeenth century, the Jewish community of New York can be

cat. 33 (detail)

fairly described as an established and slowly growing
one. While worship still took place in private spaces, a
Torah scroll had been donated and a cemetery
established, the two essential requirements for any new
Jewish community (besides, that is, the presence of a
sufficient number of Jews, presumably for a minyan of
ten adult males).

One of the most important aspects of life for the new
community in the future United States was that, unlike
in Europe, the Jews did not represent—by any
means—a uniquely disadvantaged religious
community. Nor were they perceived as dangerous to
the general order, in the way that Christians could be. In
the seventeenth and eighteenth centuries, in the wake
of the Reformation and the European wars of religion,
the leaders of the Protestant-ruled Dutch and English
colonies saw much greater danger in the Roman
Catholics and Lutherans than they did in the Jews.
Further, the religious establishments—first the Dutch
Calvinists, then the Anglicans—were more alarmed by
extreme Protestant dissidents, such as the Quakers,
than they were by the Jews. This meant that even if the
Jews could not feel completely at ease in their new
homes, at least they were able to appear no more alien,
and less threatening, than other groups. The notion of a
specific American Jewish identity lay generations in the
future, but the openness of New Netherlands/New York
and some other colonies to Jewish immigration—
admittedly sometimes stated in terms of encouraging

economic development, and keeping in mind the fact
that the communities were very small indeed—
suggested that this would become a real choice.

The Library's possessions on early Dutch New
Amsterdam and English New York include the notes
and documents preserved by a contemporary local
Dutch official (cat. 26–30) and a number of important
maps and images.

cat. 25

cat. 25

Peter (Petrus) Stuyvesant
(1611/12–1672)
Steel engraving by Charles Kennedy Burt (1823–1892)
New York, nineteenth century

The Hans Bontemantel Collection (cat. 26–30)
Hans Bontemantel (1613–1688) was a merchant and official
in New Amsterdam. He is chiefly remembered in historical
studies for the notes he preserved about ongoing government
operations and conflicts in New Amsterdam, taken from
contemporary documents. Although these notes do not
provide a comprehensive picture of developments, they
often illustrate the changes and conflicts.

cat. 26

Peter (Petrus) Stuyvesant
Letter to West India Company directors, October 30, 1655

Peter Stuyvesant, the Director-General of the New Netherland colony, was opposed to allowing Jews or Christians other than Dutch Calvinists to settle and do business in the colony. He wrote: "Jewish liberty here is very detrimental, because the Christians cannot compete against them; and if they receive liberty, the Lutherans and papists cannot be refused." The company directors rejected his views, partly in order to encourage settlement and business in the colony, but also presumably because Jews were among the company's shareholders in the Netherlands.

cat. 27

Peter (Petrus) Stuyvesant
Letter to West India Company directors, June 10, 1656

Despite the West India Company's rejection of his views, Stuyvesant begins this letter: "Concerning the Jewish nation, as far as trade is concerned they are not hindered, but trade here with the same privileges and liberties as other inhabitants. They have many times petitioned us for the free and public exercise of their abominable religion. Time will show what [rights and privileges] they can obtain from Your Honors."

cat. 28

Resolution of the High Mighty Lords States-General
Amsterdam, January 29, 1657
Page: 1

As a director, Bontemantel was involved in cleaning up the issues remaining from the West India Company's hasty withdrawal from Brazil. Jacob Valverde, once one of Recife's chief Jewish merchants, was allowed "to plead before the Court of Holland concerning the revision for annulment of the judgment pronounced by the [defunct] Council of Brazil."

cat. 29

New Netherland Council
Report to the West India Company Directors, 1657–58, July 23, 1658

This annual report refers to one of the most important documents in the history of religious freedom in the future United States, the Flushing Remonstrance. The report states: "[T]he village of Vlissingen [now Flushing] on Long Island gave the Director [Stuyvesant] an insolent reply in refusing to obey the order to expel the Quakers, saying that they regard themselves as morally obliged and legally entitled to lodge them. The matter has been taken care of and punishment meted out." The original document has been lost, but its defense of worship survived not only in the history of freedom of religion for

Extract uyt de Generale Missive uyt Nieu-middelborgh
den 30 Octob 1655. geteyken bij Pieter
Stuyvesant Nicolaes de Sille la montagne
... ordonnance van de fiscael ... Generael en
Raeds borgers van Bresijl.

de wegens de ... ... wegens de ... ...

...

...

...

...

...

...

...

...

Rekening wegens Cornelis Osborn.

...

cat. 26

De franse capit.
Baulieu
comt met een
spaense prys op d'...

De franse capit. Baulieu comt met de spaense prys op de
...rivier, becomt confere te ...

t'gepasseerde wegens de ... op langs eylant.

gepasseerde wegens
des ... op
langer eylant

Requas de predicanten en Burgemeesters ... ... van niew
Amsterdam, ... de hulptlijcke predicant Johannes ... gat ...

... vrouw om ... ...

James groot come met brieff uyt Engelant van Cromwel die
wil inde dorps op lange eylant des leefs, de maystraes ...
be ... leeds de brief ..., die ... ...   Augustus
1657.

hulptlijcke predicant ... ... te ...

... wilt hem hysbraech gedaen ... gestoorlis ... ...
pardonneert. 8 Octob. 1657

Gideon
... Schaets
predicae inde
Coll. ... ...
op ... ...
... ordere
... ...
... 624

Domine gidron schaets predicaen inde Collonie van Rensselaers
wyck, woort predicaen over ... oranje en dorp Beverwyck op
versouck de selve gemeente, sal hebben hondert gulden smaens
alles op approbatie der Heeren ...   10 Octob. 1657.

Jan ... ... gemaeckt Commies op de Zuyt Revier ... de
Comp: Jurisdictie.

placaet wegens de reductie des Zeewans ... ... der
... ... gulders, zeewan van acht ... witte van der stuyver
... het braese van 3 tot 4, voor de stuyck, op des Comps. comtoir
23 novemb. 1657.

Het ... house ... geplaeckte scheepsvrack afgekeurt volgens
voor ... gestelde ordre van ... brieven ... de huys van ...
... brieff of ... gedaen te ... in Zeewan om 150 leers smanes
te ... uyt ... ... leers te ladens ...   15 decemb
1657.

Het dorps vlissinge op lange eylant antwoorde ... ... des ...
niet willende ... ... uyt haer de quaekers, met ... ...
te ... ... ordre, ... straffe dat in gedaen.

ordre op de leer... des huys van Amsterdam, die te leers ... de
15 ...; de ... ... de ... ofte ... om ...
... gedaen te ..., voor ... ... de ... ...
dat de ... ...   15 Januari 1658.

Ordre op ... ..., moest ... ... de proclamatie de gehoude
... 15 ... 1658.

fig. 5
"View of Flushing (Long Island) North America. Mr Bowne's house. It remains in the possession of his family ever since 1661 time when it was built." Lithograph by Charles Etienne Pierre Motte (1785–1836) after the painting by Jacques Gérard Milbert (1766–1840), [1825]

fig. 5

Quakers, but for other faiths as well, although it was couched in terms of fervent Christian religious belief. This document served as an early signpost on the road to full religious freedom, along with certain colonial and later state and the U.S. constitutions:

You have been pleased to send up unto us a certain prohibition or command that we should not receive or entertain any of those people called Quakers because they are supposed to be by some, seducers of the people. For our part we cannot condemn them in this case, neither can we stretch out our hands against them, to punish, banish or persecute them for out of Christ God is a consuming fire, and it is a fearful thing to fall into the hands of the living God. . . . The law of love, peace and liberty in the states extending to Jews, Turks, and Egyptians, as they are considered the sonnes of Adam, which is the glory of the outward state of Holland, soe love, peace and liberty, extending to all in Christ Jesus, condemns hatred, war and bondage. And because our Saviour sayeth it is impossible but that offences will come, but woe unto him by whom they cometh, our desire is not to offend

one of his little ones, in whatsoever form, name or title he appears in, whether Presbyterian, Independent, Baptist or Quaker, but shall be glad to see anything of God in any of them, desiring to doe unto all men as we desire all men should doe unto us, which is the true law both of Church and State; for our Saviour sayeth this is the law and the prophets.

The local authorities were again overruled by West India Company directors. In fact the directors' instruction to Stuyvesant, a few years later, is telling. In the light of the overwhelming need to encourage immigration and economic development, he was advised to "allow every one to have his own belief, as long as he behaves quietly and legally, gives no offence to his neighbors and does not oppose the government."[2] John Bowne (1627–1695), a farmer who had emigrated from England and allowed the Quakers to worship in his home, went to the Netherlands and accomplished this turn of events. Bowne's house is now a protected historical site in Flushing, in Queens, New York.

cat. 30

Nicasius de Sille (ca. 1610–1674)
Census of New Amsterdam, July 10, 1660
Pages: 1–2

Nicasius de Sille was the *Schout* (Sheriff) of New Amsterdam. This census counted 342 buildings in New Amsterdam and shows their distribution over 28 streets. The city institutions listed are the Latin school, brewery, fiscal's garden, fort, church, cemetery, city hall, slaughterhouse, fish market, weighing house, hospital, West India Company warehouses, and gallows. There is no reference to any Jewish-owned home or other building, although a few Jews lived and worked there at this time.

cat. 30a

Lijste vande opgenomen Huijs
op den 10 Julij 1660: binnen
deser Stede Amsterdam
in N: Nederlant

De Bever Straet daer Burgermr Crigier woont Zijndt geteldt	51 huijsen
De Bever dwars Straet is tussens 't Latijtsche School	0
Bijten de Bever poort op de Paede twee huijsen	9
De prince straet daer de fiscaels Tijnck straet, Zijn	24
De prince Straet is de Bouwerijs van de Rood Leuw	5
De Tijn Straet daer de fiscael Tijn straet	1
De Smee Straet daer notaris Schelluijn woont ...	16
Het Stich Strijt daer Clerck Drijsingh woont	6
De Smeets daer koopman woont	17
De Waeter poort	
Op de Waell daer Sr G... Couwenhoven woont van Boorden, Zijn	23
De Hoogh Straet daer de notaris van ... woont	25
De Beer Straet daer Jacob ... Haecks woont	23
De Winckel Straet daer Volckert Woutersz woont	14
Het marckt Veldt daer Cornelis Quick woont	10
Het marck veldt Langs daer Antonis woont	9
De Brouwers Straet daer Borgermr ... Cortlant woont	10
De Winckel Straet daer de fiscael woont Zijn	6
De Brouwers Bruch bij Hendrick Jansz vander ...	
De Brouwers Bruch bij Jacob van Couwenhoven	
De Brief Straet daer Schout Hendrick Kip woont	
Opt Waell daer Strijt Jansz Burgermr de Commandeur woont	10
De Paede Straet daer ... Couwenhoven woont	20
De Heijren Bruch daer Dirck Jansz woont	2
Simmettuijts Bruch daer Govert ... Brost woont Zijn	5
De Kroon Bitter Bier de Smitt Gelli Bert	24
Op de Paede tijden van de Brouckstr Zijn	2
Op de Waell binnen daer D: ... Drijsi Burgermr staen Zijn	4
Somma	**342**

cat. 30b

Het Casteel Amsterdam staet op Tinijs Tanck's Boogh
De wint Mooln van ...
De Compagnies tuijn op De Bever Straet
De Kerck int Casteel
De Kerckhoff op De Bever Straet
De Stadt Prijs staet op De Waell
De Waell inde Hoogh Straet achter Het Stadt Prijs
De Vis marckt op De Waell voor Hendrick Jansze vander Vin
De Waell op Het Waelde tussens De Wijnbruch die op Het Waelde, inde Vocht is
De Galt Prijs is inde Bever Straet achter de fiscaels Prijs

de 5 huijsen vande Compagnie staen inde Winckel Straet.

Het gherecht op het casteel

Namen van alle plaetsen in Nieuw Nederlandt onder het Contoir der Lande Westindische Compe

Plaetsen	Durps
Het Casteel Amsterdam	Breukelen
de Stadt Amsterdam	Midwoudt
Het fort Oragne	Vlissingen
de Stadt Beverwijck	Middelburg
de Colonij Rinselaers wijck	Heemstede
Het fort Altena	Aernhem
de Colonij Nieuw Amstel	Vtrecht
de Colonij vande Swedn Timmecong	Haerlem
	Amersfoort
	Rustdurp
	Asopis
	Grave Sande
	Vostdurp

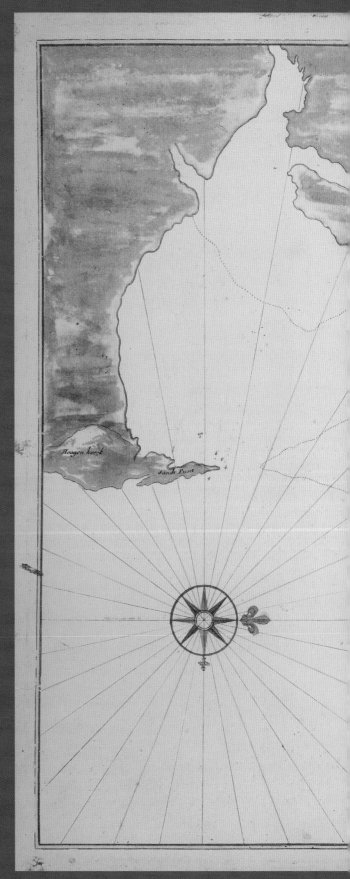

**New Amsterdam, New York, and Vicinity
in Early Images and Maps**

The Americas and the new colonies were favorite
subjects of mapmakers and illustrators; copies and
variants were often made, making them difficult to date
and attribute. New Amsterdam/New York and the
surrounding territories were especially popular and are
well represented in The New York Public Library's
collections.

cat. 31

"De Manatus, op de Noort Rivier" (Manhattan Island
on the North [Hudson] River), 1639
Full-size photograph of the Manatus map in the
Medicea-Laurenziana Library in Florence, known as the
Castello copy

This 1639 map is the earliest attempt to portray
Manhattan and its environs. It may have been drawn by
Johannes Vingboons, cartographer to the Prince of
Nassau for the West India Company. It depicts
plantations, farms, sawmills, slave quarters, and a few
roads and villages in what is now Brooklyn.

cat. 31

REDRAFT
of
THE CASTELLO PLAN
NEW AMSTERDAM
in
1660

JOHN WOLCOTT ADAMS
I.N. PHELPS STOKES
1916

cat. 32

Castello plan of New Amsterdam, 1660, redrafted
1916
Proof sheet of plate in I.N.P. Stokes's *The Iconography of
Manhattan Island, 1498–1909* (1915–28)

The original plan was prepared by Jacques Cortelyou,
surveyor of New Amsterdam, in 1660. It was sold shortly
thereafter, with other images, to Cosimo III de' Medici;
more than two hundred years later it was found in the
Villa di Castello near Florence, hence its name. The 1916
version reproduced here, which adds many streets and
other locations to the original, was created by I. N.
Phelps Stokes for his monumental six-volume
Iconography of Manhattan Island.

cat. 33

cat. 33

Novum Amsterodamum (New Amsterdam)
Engraving, 1671

This view of the New Amsterdam port is most likely taken from a sketch made by Laurens Hermansz. Block, an artist who visited aboard a mercantile ship in either 1650 or 1651. While there are merely a few dozen buildings present in this image (windmills, gallows, homes), contemporaneous descriptions and maps of the area show several hundred structures, a significant city in early colonial America.

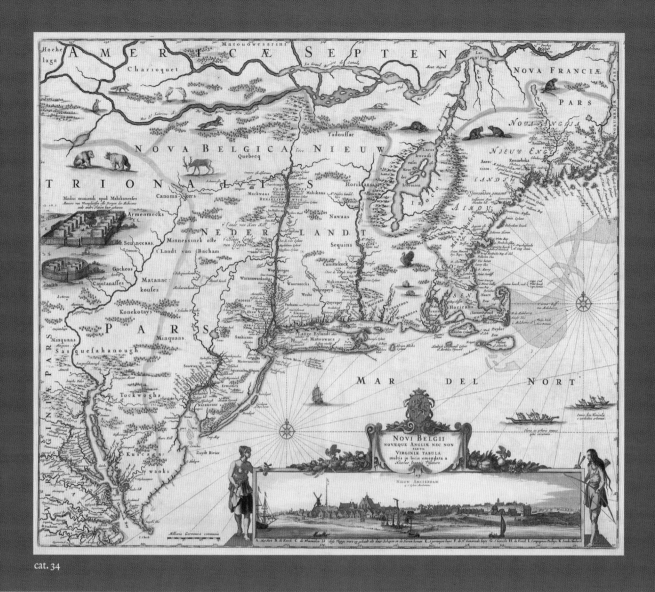

cat. 34

cat. 34

Novi Belgii Novaeque Angliae nec non partis Virginiae tabula multis in locis emendata (Map of the New Netherlands and New England as well as part of Virginia, with many corrections)
Hand-colored engraving published by Nicolaes Visscher, ca. 1651–55

Although derived primarily from existing Dutch cartography, this map makes some important updates to Europe's understanding of the New Netherlands

colony, including the depiction of Long Island as a single feature. It is most notable, however, for being one of the earliest known views of the city of New Amsterdam. The map was also later used by James, Duke of York, to determine the boundaries between New York and New Jersey upon the latter's formation.

69

cat. 35

Nieu Amsterdam at. New York (New Amsterdam and New York)
Hand-colored engraving from Carel Allard, *Orbis habitabilis oppida et vestitus* (The towns and costumes of the inhabited world) (Amsterdam, 1710)

This rare allegorical view, engraved in 1710 by Aldert Meyer, was included among the one hundred views of cities and their inhabitants in Carel Allard's *Orbis habitabilis oppida et vestitus* (The towns and costumes of the inhabited world) (Amsterdam, 1710). The city, showing signs of its decades of growth under European habitation, is flanked by two Native American residents, presumably of the Lenni Lenape tribe who occupied the area.

Notes

1. Leo Hershowitz, "By Chance or Choice: Jews in New Amsterdam 1654," *American Jewish Archives* 57 (2005): 1–13, describes and analyzes the archival information in detail.
2. Edward Tanjore Corwin, ed., *Ecclesiastical Records, State of New York* (Albany: Hugh Hastings, State Historian, 1901–16), 1: 530.

NIEU AMSTERDAM al. NEW YORK

ordinum Hollandiæ & Westfrisiæ

een Mahakuaes Indiaen, met hun Steden en woningen

Et Landt alhier is in 't gemeyn gelijck in Hoog-duytslandt / het Landt
goet en seer lijftochtig van alles / dat tot des Menschen lijf noodig is / uyt-
gesondert het Habijt/ Linnen/ Wollen/ Koussen/ Schoenen/ &c. Die va

4

Jewish Indians, Puritans and Quakers, the Christian Millennium, and the *Hope of Israel*

One of the strangest—and mostly now forgotten—pieces of early American intellectual and religious history was the notion that the native population of the Americas represented the Ten Lost Tribes of ancient Israel. It is a theory that exercised many of the best minds of the seventeenth century, and has never completely disappeared. While it is not, properly speaking, part of the history of the Jews in America, it is certainly an important element in the study of the historical Christian perception of the Jewish place in the New World.

Now the idea seems absurd. But what was—or is—this theory? An American historian has noted, "Whenever I tell students in America that there was a serious theory years ago that the Indians were Jews, and that some of the lost tribes were located in America, they look blankly at me as if it's my nonsense, or they laugh embarrassedly to be in a room where such things are said."[1]

First, the "lost tribes" were ten of the twelve traditional tribes of Israel—all except the tribes of Judah and Benjamin. According to the Second Book of Kings, the Assyrians, after conquering the northern kingdom of Israel, deported to the East some part of the population made up of the ten tribes—in fact, the account is not very clear or definite. (The southern kingdom of Judah, centered in Jerusalem and representing the other two tribes, survived for another couple of centuries until it, too, was conquered.) The Ten Lost Tribes eventually became the focus of much

heated controversy and theorizing—did they still exist as tribes, or even as nations or kingdoms? If so, where? How far to the east? Many ideas were advanced and discoveries proclaimed. But the fundamental assumption that they must still exist remained a powerful one.

It was certainly a serious concept when the discoveries of Columbus and other explorers opened the American continents for European settlement and exploitation. Confronted with previously unknown populations—the American Indians of both North and South America, as well as native peoples of the islands of the Caribbean—European Christians, imbued with a profoundly religious world view, had to find a place for them in this view; it had to be, moreover, derived from the Christian version of the Hebrew scriptures. In brief, how could the American Indians fit into the Hebrew Bible? If it was thought that all people descended from the Adam and Eve of the book of Genesis, how exactly could the Indians, whose existence was previously unsuspected and whose connections were uncertain, be included? One common answer, perhaps the most important, was that they were, or were descended from, the Ten Lost Tribes. Evidence included purported knowledge of Hebrew among the Indians, or at least relationships between their languages and Hebrew, and alleged cultural and social similarities.

In the mid-seventeenth century, among Protestant dissidents in the English-speaking world, speculation

fig. 9 (detail)

around this idea became particularly intense, including among radical Puritans and the Quakers. One reason for this was the millennial expectation that agitated the European world in the mid-seventeenth century; many Christians and Jews alike were certain that the eschatological last days were at hand—the question was exactly when, and whose religion would triumph. The Christians argued that the Jews—lost tribes and the rest—necessarily were about to convert to Christianity, at which point Christianity would triumph and the world be redeemed by Christ. On their side, many Jews saw a sign in the figure of the self-proclaimed Jewish messiah Shabbethai Tzevi as the purported hope and redeemer of Israel (see chapter 2).

Two Jews from Portuguese New Christian backgrounds, meanwhile, played important and interlocked roles. Antonio (Aaron Levi) de Montezinos was a trader who claimed to have found, in Spanish South America in the 1640s, members of the lost tribe of Reuben. He took his tale to the Jewish community in Amsterdam, where one of the community's rabbis, Manasseh ben Israel, took down his statement and subsequently wrote a book that drew on it, titled *Hope of Israel* in its different editions (*Mikveh Israel* in Hebrew, and *Spes Israelis* in Latin) (cat. 42–43). Manasseh had good connections with English Puritan intellectuals and clergymen, among them Thomas Thorowgood (cat. 40), Nathaniel Holmes, Moses Wall (cat. 43), and John Dury (cat. 39), who publicized this exciting find. They

and others proclaimed that this, the rediscovery of the lost tribes, meant that the Jews as a whole should immediately convert—presumably, to Puritan Protestant Christianity—and thereby hasten the Millennium. Manasseh, however, was not at all inclined to promote Christian messianism, and had hopes that the Jewish messiah would soon come. The rabbi was, moreover, interested in using his connections to open England to legal and open Jewish settlement.

While the 1650–60s represented the high point of the Jewish Indian theory, it continued to surface through the eighteenth century, including in the works of native-born American Protestant writers. It is noteworthy that in the nineteenth century the bases for the argument generally changed. As religion declined as the basis for the greater world view, alleged physical evidence came to be more frequently cited, for example, in reports of Jewish ritual items found in ancient graves in North America. The linguistic argument was mostly abandoned, with the progress of the study of historical linguistics proving that no possible relation existed between Hebrew and Native American languages. A sad and strange coda to the theme came at the time of the Chinese Boxer Rebellion in 1900. A Jewish immigrant to Boston, Uziel Haga, begged President McKinley to allow him to accompany the American expeditionary force to China, because Haga was convinced that the lost tribes would be found there. McKinley agreed he could go, but then

Haga disappeared in China, probably killed by Chinese revolutionaries.[2]

The idea has never entirely disappeared. A form appears in Mormon (Church of Latter Day Saints) religious literature. An internet search will quickly turn up adherents of various versions, still arguing over specifics.

Regardless, the Jewish Indian theory is important in the development of American identity. For Christians, it placed the Native Americans of North and South America firmly within the familiar context of the Christian understanding of Hebrew scripture. For Americans in particular, it could be used to suggest an American role in Christian messianic visions. Among Jews, the emphasis was different. The interest displayed by Manasseh ben Israel, for example, must be seen against the background of the overwhelming Jewish tragedy of the expulsions and forced conversions of the Jews of Spain and Portugal, and the subsequent rebuilding of Jewish identity and community in the expanding Atlantic world.[3]

cat. 36

John Udall (ca. 1560–1592)

מפתח לשון הקדש

Mafteah leshon ha-kodesh, that is, The Key of the Holy Tongue.
Wherein is conteineid, first the Hebrue Grammar (in a manner)
woord for woord out of P. Martinius . . .
Leyden: Francis Raphelengius, 1593
Page: Title page

This is the first Hebrew grammar printed in English,
though it is basically an abridged translation of the
Grammatica Hebraea of Pierre Martinez (Petrus Martinius),
originally published 1568 and republished several times.
John Udall was an early English Puritan clergyman. He
ends the book with the words in Hebrew, "Written by
Yohanan [John] Udall in jail." Udall was imprisoned for
his attacks on the established Anglican church, and he
died before the book was published.

cat. 37

The Whole Booke of Psalmes, Faithfully Translated into
English Metre. Whereunto Is Prefixed a Discourse Declaring
Not Only the Lawfullnes, But Also the Necessity of the Heavenly
Ordinance of Singing Scripture Psalmes in the Churches of God
Cambridge, Mass: S. Daye, 1640. Translated by Richard
Mather, John Eliot, and Thomas Weld
Page: Title page
Page: 3 ("Preface"), displaying the first use of Hebrew type
in America

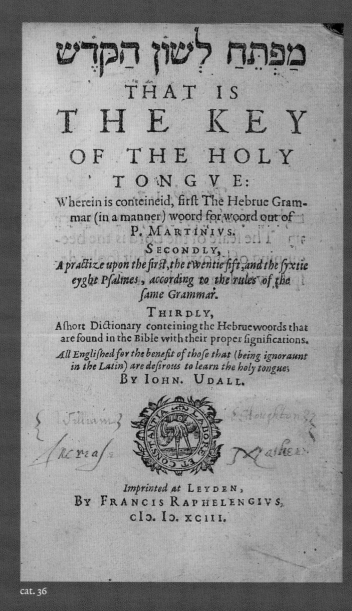

cat. 36

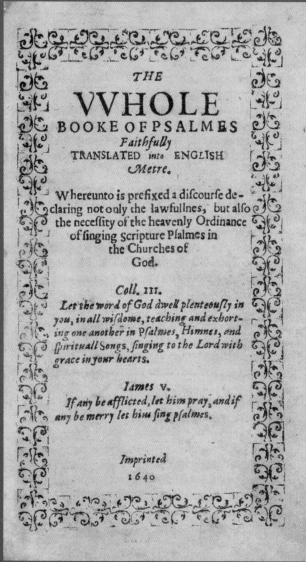

THE

VVHOLE

BOOKE OF PSALMES

Faithfully
TRANSLATED *into* ENGLISH
Metre.

Whereunto is prefixed a difcourfe declaring not only the lawfullnes, but alfo
the neceffity of the heavenly Ordinance
of finging Scripture Pfalmes in
the Churches of
God.

Coll. III.

*Let the word of God dwell plenteoufly in
you, in all wifdome, teaching and exhort-
ing one another in Pfalmes, Himnes, and
fpirituall Songs, finging to the Lord with
grace in your hearts.*

Iames V.

*If any be afflicted, let him pray, and if
any be merry let him fing pfalmes.*

Imprinted
1640

---

members, but the whole Church is commaund-
ed to teach one another in all the feverall forts
of Davids pfalmes, fome being called by himfelfe
מזמורים : pfalms, fome תהילים Hymns
fome שירים : fpirituall fongs. foe that if the
finging Davids pfalmes be a morall duty & ther-
fore perpetuall, then wee under the new Teftamēt
are bound to fing them as well as they under the
old : and if wee are exprefly commanded to fing
Pfalmes, Hymnes, and fpirituall fongs, then either
wee muft fing Davids pfalmes, or elfe may affirm
they are not fpirituall fongs: which being penned
by an extraordiary gift of the Spirit, for the fake
efpecially of Gods fpirituall Ifraell, not to be
read and preached only (as other parts of holy
writ) but to be fung alfo, they are therefore moft
fpirituall, and ftill to be fung of all the Ifraell of
God: and verily as their fin is exceeding great,
who will allow Davids pfalmes (as other fcrip-
tures) to be read in churches (which is one end)
but not to be preached alfo, (which is another end
foe their fin is crying before God, who will allow them to be read and preached, but feeke to
deprive the Lord of the glory of the third end of
them, which is to fing them in chriftian churches.
obj. 1 If it be fayd that the Saints in the primi-
tive Church did compile fpirituall fongs of their
owne inditing, and fing them before the Church.
1 Cor. 14, 15, 16.
Anf. We anfwer firft, that thofe Saints compiled
thefe fpirituall fongs by the extraordinary gifts of
the

* 3

Known as the Bay Psalm Book from its origin in the Massachusetts Bay Colony, this is the first book printed in English within the confines of the future continental United States. These metrical but unpoetical versions were produced by the "chief Divines" of the Bay Colony, John Cotton (1584–1662), Richard Mather (1596–1669), John Eliot (1604–1690), and Thomas Weld (1590?–1662). Arguably *the* icon of American printing history, the Bay Psalm Book is not a beautiful book. It is printed indifferently, using types brought from England in 1638, but it displays the first use of Hebrew type in America, cut specially for this book.

cat. 38

John Eliot (1604–1690)
The Holy Bible Containing the Old Testament and the New. Translated into the Indian Language and Ordered to Be Printed by the Commissioners of the United Colonies in New-England, at the Charge, and with the Consent of the Corporation in England for the Propagation of the Gospel Amongst the Indians in New-England
Cambridge, Mass.: Samuel Green & Marmaduke Johnson, 1663
Page: Title page

This work, often referred to as the Eliot Indian Bible, was the first Bible printed in America and was intended to be used for the conversion to Puritan Christianity of native

peoples around the Massachusetts Bay Colony. The language is Algonquian. The first English-language Bibles were not published in the American colonies until the eighteenth century. Conventional wisdom holds that the version with the English additions, including supplemental title pages to the Old and New Testaments, was intended to demonstrate to the English king and Parliament that their funds supporting missionary work were being used wisely. This edition, with a long dedicatory preface to King Charles II, is encountered infrequently. Eliot was the outstanding figure among early Puritan Christian missionaries in Massachusetts.

cat. 39

Edward Winslow (1595–1655)
The Glorious Progress of the Gospel, Amongst the Indians in New England. Manifested by Three Letters ... With an Appendix ... By J. D. Minister of the Gospel
London: Printed for Hannah Allen in Popes-head-alley, 1649
Page: Title page

In his "Epistle Dedicatory," Winslow links two great questions: "What became of the Ten Tribes of Israel?" and "Where did the American Indians come from?" The author of the appendix, "J. D. Minister of the Gospel," was John Dury (1596–1680), one of the leading Puritan millenarians. Dury claimed that "the wisest Jews now

THE

HOLY BIBLE:

CONTAINING THE

OLD TESTAMENT

AND THE *NEW*.

Translated into the

INDIAN LANGUAGE,

AND

Ordered to be Printed by the *Commissioners of the United Colonies*
in *NEW-ENGLAND*,

At the Charge, and with the Consent of the

CORPORATION IN ENGLAND

For the Propagation of the Gospel amongst the Indians
in New-England.

CAMBRIDGE:

Printed by *Samuel Green* and *Marmaduke Johnson*.

MDCLXIII.

cat. 38

THE

Glorious Progress

OF THE

GOSPEL,

AMONGST THE

Indians in New England.

MANIFESTED

By three Letters, under the Hand of that famous Instrument of the Lord Mr. JOHN ELIOT,
And another from Mr. *Thomas Mayhew* jun: both Preachers of
the Word, as well to the *English* as *Indians* in *New England*.

WHEREIN

The riches of Gods Grace in the effectuall calling of
many of them is cleared up: As also a manifestation of the hungring
desires of many People in sundry parts of that Country, after the
more full Revelation of the Gospel of *Jesus Christ*, to the
exceeding Consolation of every Christian Reader.

TOGETHER,

With an Appendix to the foregoing Letters, holding forth Conjectures, Observations, and Applications.
By *I. D.* Minister of the Gospell.

Published by EDWARD WINSLOW.

Mal. 1. 11. *From the rising of the Sun, even unto the going down of the
same, my Name shall be great among the Gentiles, and in every place in-
cense shall be offered unto my Name, and a pure Offering ; for my Name
shall be great among the Heathen, saith the Lord of Hosts.*

LONDON, Printed for *Hannah Allen* in *Popes-head-Alley*. 1649.

cat. 39

living" (unnamed, but presumably including Manasseh ben Israel, whom Dury knew) believe "that about the year 1650, *Either we Christians shall be Mosaick* [i.e., Jewish], *or else that they themselves Jewes shall be Christians*" (p. 22). The presumed outcome in the minds of the Christian divines was, of course, the latter case. Dury connects the missionary activities in New England among the Indians with the expected conversion of all Jews—lost tribes and the rest.

cat. 40

Thomas Thorowgood (ca. 1600–ca. 1669)
Jewes in America, or, Probabilities that the Americans Are of that Race. With the Removall of Some Contrary Reasonings, and Earnest Desires for Effectuall Endeavours to Make Them Christian
London: Printed by W. H. for T. Slater, 1650
Page: Title page

Thorowgood, a minister in the rural English county of Norfolk, attempted to identify customs common to American Indians and Biblical Jews; for example, "They delight exceedingly in dancing, men and women, yea and women apart by themselves. And so they did in Israel (Exodus 13:20)." He also finds similarities between Hebrew and Indian languages. Antonio (Aaron Levi) de Montezinos's statement appears at the end of the book. However, the preface, "An epistolicall

discourse of Mr. John Dury, to Mr. Thorowgood," includes correspondence between Dury, another English millenarian, Nathaniel Holmes (or Homes), and Manasseh ben Israel. Thorowgood did not give up on his arguments. Two years later he produced a closely related work under the title *Digitus dei: New Discoveryes with Sure Arguments to Prove that the Jews (a Nation) or People Lost in the World for the Space of Near 200 [sic] Years, Inhabite Now in America*. The next edition, of 1660, *Jews in America, or Probabilities, that Those Indians Are Judaical, Made More Probable by Some Additionals to the Former Conjectures*, contained Thorowgood's exchanges with John Eliot himself as the expert on Indians.

cat. 41

Rembrandt van Rijn (1606–1669)
Manasseh ben Israel
Etching, Amsterdam, 1636

Manasseh ben Israel (1604–1657) was born, as Manoel Dias Soeiro, on the island of Madeira into a converso family; the family moved to the Netherlands a few years later. Though he served as one of the rabbis of the Portuguese synagogue in Amsterdam, he became well known in British intellectual circles. He published in Latin and Spanish as well as Hebrew, and corresponded with British millenarians who fervently pressed him to concede that the Jews, including, of course, the

Iewes in America,
OR,
PROBABILITIES
That the AMERICANS are of
that Race.

With the removall of some
contrary reasonings, and earnest desires for effectuall endeavours to
make them Christian.

Proposed by THO: THOROVVGOOD, B. D. one of the
Assembly of Divines.

CANT. 8. 8. *We have a little sister, and she hath no breasts, what*
shall we doe for our sister in the day when she shall be spoken for?
MAT. 8. 11. *Many shall come from the East, and from the West,*
and shall sit downe with Abraham, *and* Isaac, *and* Jacob *in the*
Kingdome of Heaven.

Æthiopes vertuntur in filios Dei, si egerint pænitentiam, &
filii Dei. transeunt in Æthiopes si in profundum venerint
peccatorum : Hieronym. in Esai,

London, Printed by *W. H.* for *Tho. Slater,* and are be to sold
at his shop at the signe of the Angel in Duck lane, 1650.

cat. 40

cat. 41

purported Jewish Indians of the Americas, should convert to Christianity so as to hasten the coming of the (Christian) messiah. But he made no such concession. In 1655 he undertook a mission to convince the English to allow Jews to settle openly and legally in England, but in this he failed, returning home after two years and dying soon after. (In fact Jews were allowed thereafter to settle quietly in England.) There is a scholarly consensus that he knew the Dutch artist Rembrandt van Rijn, perhaps quite well; the artist executed illustrations for one of Manasseh ben Israel's books. Several portraits by different artists from mid-seventeenth century Amsterdam are said to depict him, but identifications are uncertain. This is one of the candidates, by Rembrandt himself.

cat. 42

Manasseh ben Israel (1604–1657)

מקוה ישראל

Mikveh Yisrael. Hoc est, Spes Israelis (That is, The hope of Israel)

Amsterdam, 1650

Page: Title page

cat. 43

Manasseh ben Israel

The Hope of Israel

Trans. with additions by Moses Wall, 2nd ed.

London: Printed by R. I. for L. Chapman, 1651

The title page of this translation by Moses Wall adds: "Whereunto are added some discourses upon the point of the conversion of the Jewes: By Moses Wall." Facing eager questions from his British correspondents, Manasseh remained cautious, though he did believe that Montezinos was sincere and that the South American tribes represented some element of the lost tribes of Israel, and that the messianic age could not be far off:

The shortness of time when we believe our redemption shall appear is confirmed by this, that the Lord hath promised that he will gather the two tribes, Judah and Benjamin, out of the four corners of the world, from whence you may gather, that for the fulfilling of that they must be scattered through all the corners of the world; as Daniel saith, "And when the scattering of the holy people shall have an end, all those things shall be fulfilled." And this appeares now to be done, when as our Synagogues are found in America (p. 42).

Within a few years, Manasseh's work appeared in Latin, Hebrew, Spanish, English, and Dutch. This English translation was by the political and religious radical millenarian Moses Wall.

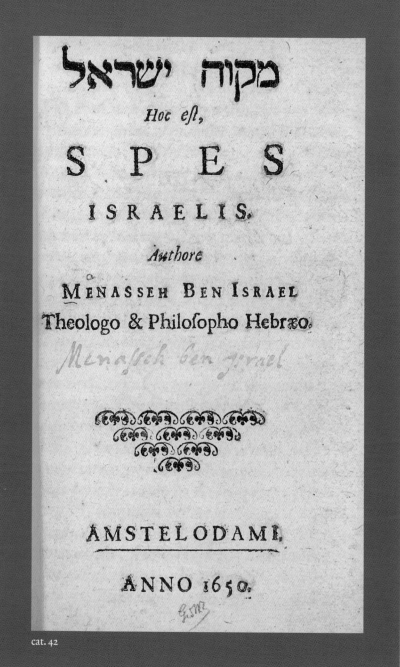

cat. 42

cat. 44

Hamon L'Estrange (1583–1654)
Americans No Iewes, or Improbabilities that the Americans are of That Race
London: Printed by W. W. for H. Seile, 1652
Page: Title page

Sir Hamon L'Estrange was a member of a leading landowning family in the county of Norfolk, and deeply involved in the tumultuous political history of his time. In this book he rebutted Thorowgood's purported proofs, one by one. He suggests, in particular, that many of the practices among the Indians that Thorowgood cites as evidence of Jewish origins are in fact ordinary human customs, "common to all ... which granted ... will make all the world Jewes" (p. 66). After finishing with Thorowgood, L'Estrange writes that he "was ready to fold up this frolique," when "there came unto mine hands a small book entitled, the Hope of *Israel* ... shewing the place of the ten Tribes ... on the South side of the ridge of the hills *Andes in Peru*." However, he knew the Andes firsthand, and "though I have often travailed over those parts on dry foot, yet I could never find the least track or trace of any matter that might invite my sense and opinion to concur with him." He describes how Manasseh "proceeds to tell a number of strange stories.... I confesse I finde him a man of so sharpe an appetite, and strong and easie and Ostrich concoction; as I cannot sit at table any longer with him, and therefore I now rise and

Americans no Iewes,

OR

Improbabilities that the *Americans* are of that race.

They shall be scattered abroad, and their remembrance shall cease. Deut. 32. v. 26.

Untill the fulnesse of the Gentiles be come in, and so all Israel shall be saved. Rom 11. 25.

For through their fall Salvation commeth to the Gentiles, to provoke them to follow them. Rom. 11. 11.

By Hamon l'Estrange, K^t.

LONDON,

Printed by *W. W.* for *Henry Seile* over against St. *Dunstans Church* in *Fleetstreet.* 1 6 5 2.

fig. 6
Portrait of William Penn, after
the 1832 painting by Henry Inman
(1801–1846), wood-engraving with
hand-coloring, 19th century

offer others every one to seed according to his own
phancie" (pp. 75–77). Responsibility for this book is often
assigned to L'Estrange's son, also named Hamon (1605–
1660), a prolific writer in the fields of theology and history.
But the title page shows the author as "knight," which
Hamon the younger was not, and at a couple of points the
text makes it clear that the older man is the author.

cat. 45

Mason Locke Weems (1759–1825)
The Life of William Penn, the Settler of Pennsylvania, the
Founder of Philadelphia, and One of the First Lawgivers in the
Colonies, Now United States, in 1682…
Philadelphia: H. C. Carey and I. Lea, 1822

William Penn (1644–1718), the founder of Pennsylvania,
was an outstanding figure in the development of the
Religious Society of Friends, or Quakers, into a
significant social and moral force (see cat. 60). In his
comments on Native Americans as Jews, he begins: "As
to the original of this extraordinary people [American
Indians], I cannot but believe they are of the Jewish race,
I mean of the stock of the ten tribes so long lost." After
an initial scriptural reference, Penn lists evidence: "I
find the Indians of the like countenance with the Jews;
and their children of so lively resemblance, that a man
on looking at them, would think himself in Duke's
Place, or Berry Street, London."

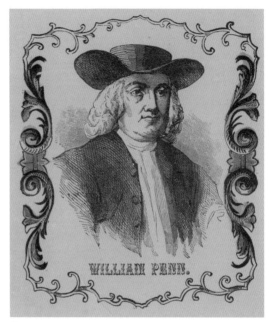

WILLIAM PENN.

fig. 6

Now spelled Bury Street, Berry Street was then a
nascent Jewish neighborhood in the northeast corner of
the City of London, home of the capital's first
synagogue, from 1657, and the Bevis Marks synagogue,
opened in 1701 and still one of the most famous
European synagogues (see the 1736 map of London,
reproduced here). Penn mentions a number of Indian
customs that he regarded as derived from Jewish ones
(pp. 183–84).

fig. 7
Urbium Londini et West-Monasterii nec non suburbii Southwark: Accurata ichnographia (An accurate plan of the cities of London and Westminster as well as the suburb of Southwark) (Nuremberg: Homann Erben, 1736). The detail view of the map shows Berry Street, Dukes Place, and the "Jews Syngogue."

fig. 7 (detail)

cat. 46

George Keith (1639?–1716)
Truth Advanced in the Correction of Many Gross & Hurtful Errors; Wherein is occasionally opened & explained many great and peculiar Mysteries and Doctrines of the Christian Religion
[New York: W. Bradford], 1694
Page: Title page

George Keith was raised Presbyterian, then became a Quaker, subsequently an aggressive dissenter from the established Philadelphia and London Friends meetings, and eventually an Anglican minister and missionary in New Jersey. A book of what may be termed apocalyptic Quakerism, *Truth Advanced* is directed toward "the Expectation of many People, both of Jews and Christians, that within a few Years, some great Alteration will come to pass in the World," as

Keith states in the "Spiritual Chronology" that concludes the book. His reckonings concerning the ages and looming end of the world are extraordinarily complex, but he is sure that, by about 1700, apocalyptic events would begin.

This was the first book published in New York. The publisher, William Bradford (1663–1752), is an outstanding figure in American printing history, working first in Philadelphia—where he had legal difficulties due to his association with Keith—and then New York, where he prospered.

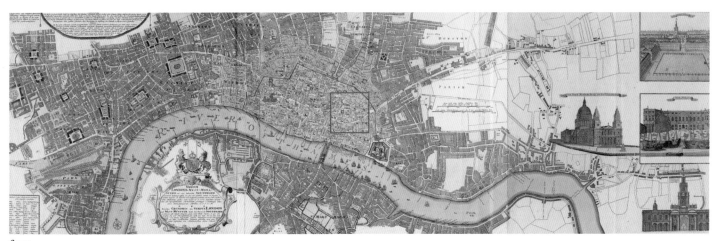

fig. 7

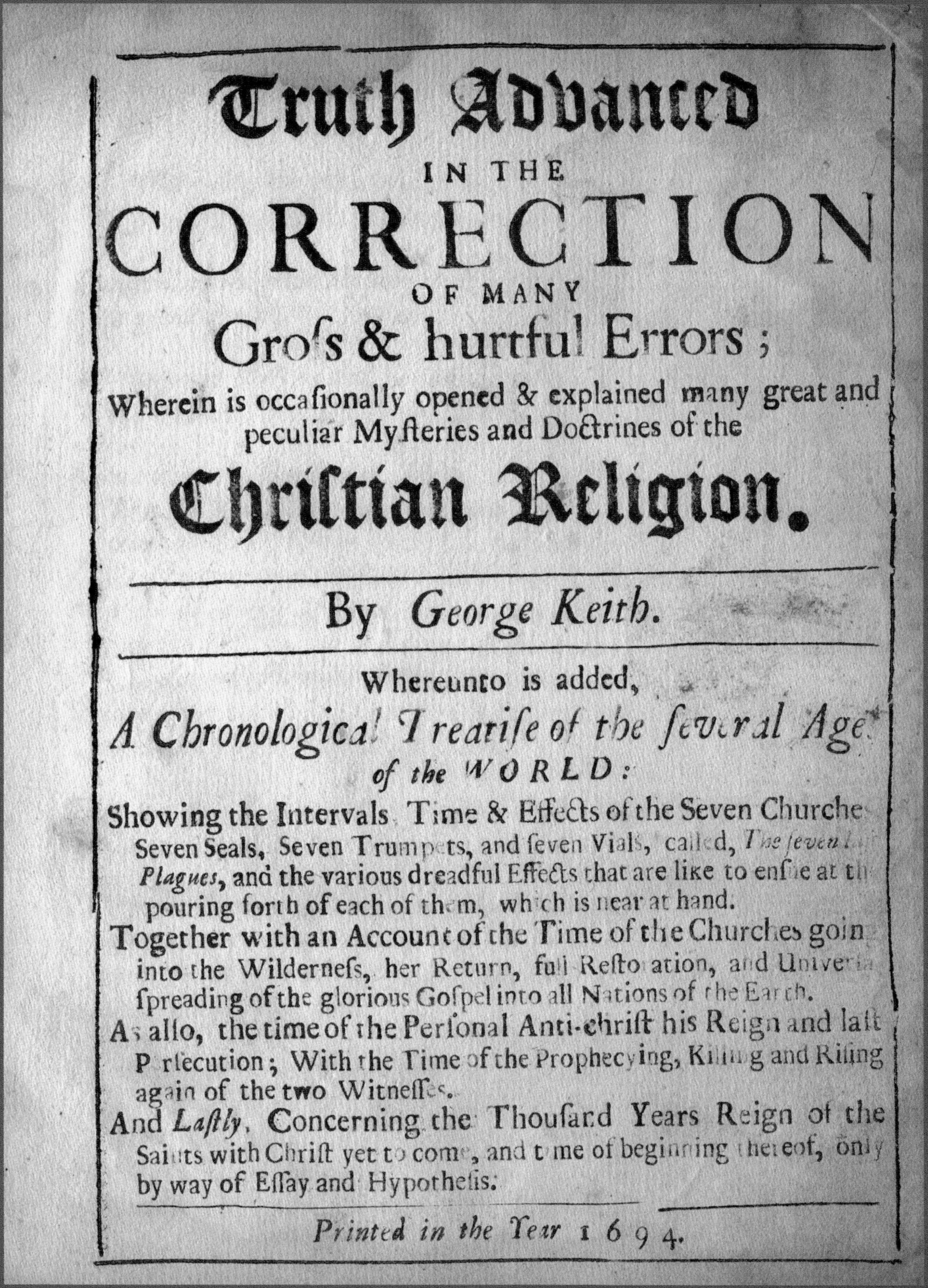

Truth Advanced

IN THE

CORRECTION

OF MANY

Gross & hurtful Errors;

Wherein is occasionally opened & explained many great and
peculiar Mysteries and Doctrines of the

Christian Religion.

By *George Keith.*

Whereunto is added,

*A Chronological Treatise of the several Ages
of the WORLD:*

Showing the Intervals, Time & Effects of the Seven Churches,
Seven Seals, Seven Trumpets, and seven Vials, called, *The seven last
Plagues,* and the various dreadful Effects that are like to ensue at the
pouring forth of each of them, which is near at hand.

Together with an Account of the Time of the Churches going
into the Wilderness, her Return, full Restoration, and Universal
spreading of the glorious Gospel into all Nations of the Earth.

As also, the time of the Personal Anti-christ his Reign and last
Persecution; With the Time of the Prophecying, Killing and Rising
again of the two Witnesses.

And *Lastly,* Concerning the Thousand Years Reign of the
Saints with Christ yet to come, and time of beginning thereof, only
by way of Essay and Hypothesis:

Printed in the Year 1694.

Emmons, N.

H. Emmons Pinx.]   O. Pelton.

The Honble. Samuel Sewall, Esqr.
Late Chief Justice of His Maj^s. Province of Massachusetts Bay in N.E.
And Judge of Probate for the County of Suffolk.

Æ. 77. 1728.

Auris, meus, oculus, manus, os, pes; munere fungi.
dum Pergunt, Praestat discere velle mori.

fig. 8

cat. 47

Samuel Sewall (1652–1730)

*Phaenomena quaedam apocalyptica ad aspectum novi orbis
configurata* (Certain apocalyptical phenomena
configured in relation to the New World). *Or, Some Few
Lines towards a Description of the New Heaven as It Makes to
Those Who Stand upon the New Earth*
Boston: Printed by B. Green and J. Allen, and to be sold
by R. Wilkins, 1697
Page: Title page

Sewall was a Harvard graduate and a judge at the Salem
witch trials—for which he later publicly apologized. In
1700 he wrote the first book attacking the American
slave trade, *The Selling of Joseph*. But the book *Phaenomena
quaedam apocalyptica* focuses on the restoration of Israel
and the coming of the millennium. He began by
suggesting that, "the *English* Nation, in shewing
Kindness to the Aboriginal Natives of *America*, may
possibly shew kindness to *Israelites* unawares" (first page
of "To the honorable Sir William Ashurst"). His view
was that the messiah would come to the Jews soon, not
in the Holy Land, but in America, since it was "manifest
to all, that very considerable Numbers of *Jews* are seated
in the New World; where they merchandize, have their
Synagogues, and places of Burial." He cites communities
in Barbados, Jamaica, Suriname, and Curaçao. Further,
"There are several Families of them at *New-York*, and *New
England* is seldom wholly without them. There were two
at *Boston, Anno* 1697, viz., Mr. *Joseph Frazon* and Mr. *Samuel*

Frazon, his brother, to whom I am beholden for a sight of
the *Spanish* Bible." Therefore, "Why may not that [i.e.,
America] be the place of *New Jerusalem*?" (p. 51). The
second edition of Sewall's book, in 1727, included as an
addendum the third edition of Samuel Willard's essay
"The Fountain Opened: Or, The Admirable Blessings
Plentifully to Be Dispensed at the National Conversion
of the Jews." Willard (1640–1707), also a Harvard
graduate and a minister in Boston, was the acting
president of Harvard College, with the official rank of
vice president from 1701 until his death.

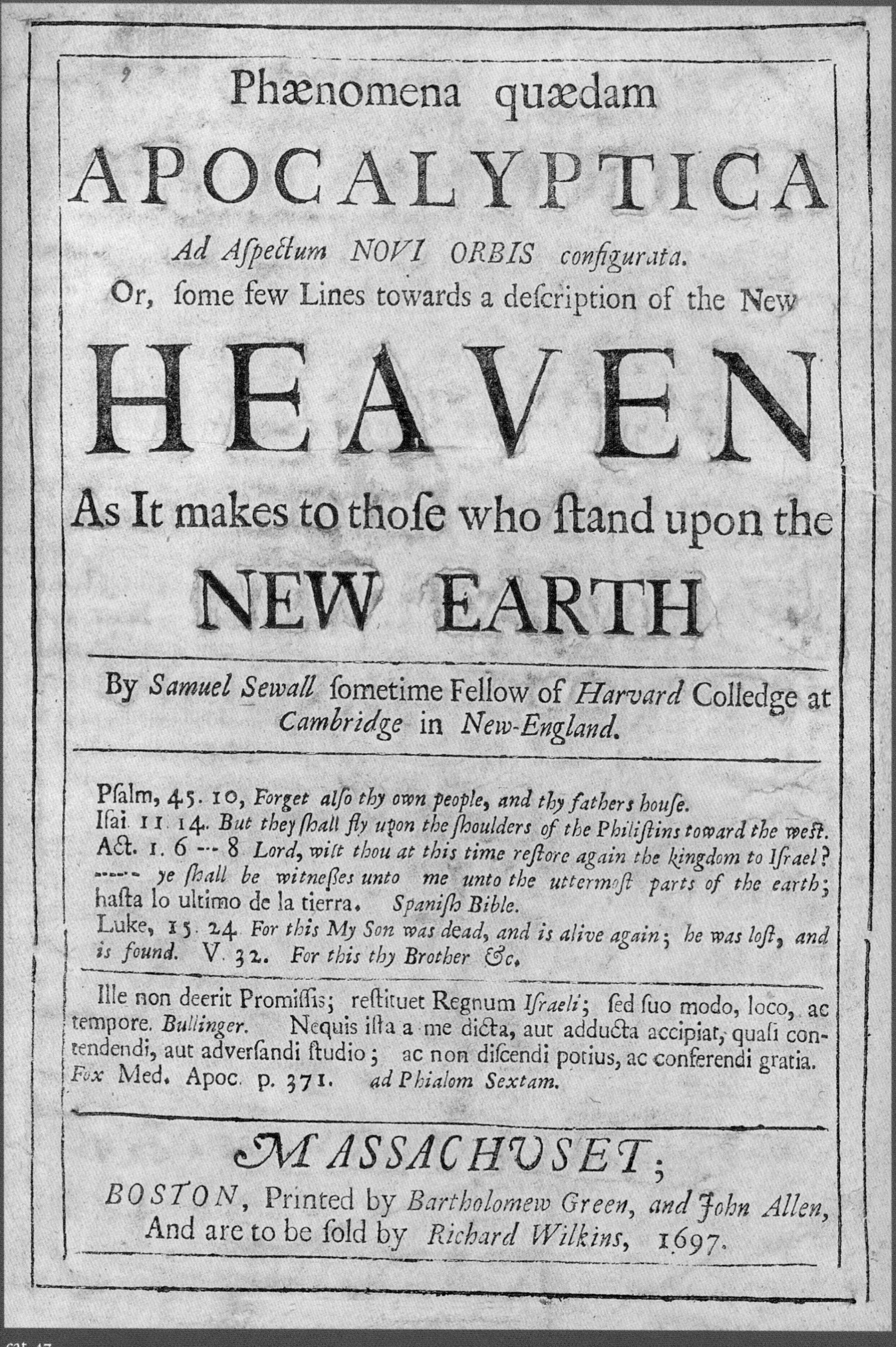

Phænomena quædam

APOCALYPTICA

Ad Aspectum NOVI ORBIS configurata.

Or, some few Lines towards a description of the New

HEAVEN

As It makes to those who stand upon the

NEW EARTH

By *Samuel Sewall* sometime Fellow of *Harvard* Colledge at *Cambridge* in *New-England*.

Psalm, 45. 10, *Forget also thy own people, and thy fathers house.*
Isai. 11. 14. *But they shall fly upon the shoulders of the Philistins toward the west.*
Act. 1. 6 --- 8 *Lord, wilt thou at this time restore again the kingdom to Israel?* ----- *ye shall be witnesses unto me unto the uttermost parts of the earth;* hasta lo ultimo de la tierra. *Spanish Bible.*
Luke, 15. 24. *For this My Son was dead, and is alive again; he was lost, and is found. V. 32. For this thy Brother &c.*

Ille non deerit Promissis; restituet Regnum *Israeli*; sed suo modo, loco, ac tempore. *Bullinger.* Nequis ista a me dicta, aut adducta accipiat, quasi contendendi, aut adversandi studio; ac non discendi potius, ac conferendi gratia. *Fox* Med. Apoc. p. 371. *ad Phialom Sextam.*

MASSACHUSET;

BOSTON, Printed by *Bartholomew Green, and John Allen,* And are to be sold by *Richard Wilkins,* 1697.

fig. 9

cat. 48

Jonathan Edwards the Younger (1745–1801)

Observations on the Language of the Muhhekaneew Indians; in Which the Extent of that Language in North-America Is Shewn; Its Genius Is Grammatically Traced: Some of Its Peculiarities, and Some Instances of Analogy between that and the Hebrew Are Pointed Out

New Haven: Printed by Josiah Meigs, 1788

Edwards, a cleric and scholar, was the son of Jonathan Edwards the Elder (d. 1758), a better-known theological and educational figure. This booklet presents a lecture given by Edwards at the Connecticut Society of Arts and Sciences in 1787 on the subject of the Muhhekaneew (Mohegan) language. Edwards was fluent from boyhood in that tongue, and familiar with other Algonquian and Iroquoian languages. Regardless of his views on similarities between Hebrew and Mohegan, he was a pioneer in the study of the historical linguistics of native North America.

fig. 10

cat. 49

Elias Boudinot (1740–1821)

A Star in the West: or, a Humble Attempt to Discover the Long Lost Ten Tribes of Israel, Preparatory to Their Return to Their Beloved City, Jerusalem

Trenton, N.J.: D. Fenton, S. Hutchinson and J. Dunham, 1816

fig. 9
"Een Mahakuase Indiaen, met
hun Steden en woningen"
(A Mohawk Indian, with their
towns and dwellings), from
*Beschrijvinghe van Virginia, Nieuw
Nederlandt, Nieuw Engelandt, en
d'eylanden Bermudes, Berbados, en
S. Christoffel. Dienstelijck voor elck een
derwaerts handelende, en alle*

voort-planters van nieuw colonien
(Description of Virginia, New
Netherlands, New England,
and the islands of Bermuda,
Barbados, and St. Kitts. For the
use of persons trading there,
and all founders of new colonies)
(Amsterdam: J. Hartgers, 1651)

fig. 10
Mezzotint portrait of Elias
Boudinot, 1798

Boudinot was a leader of the American Revolution in New Jersey, and a delegate to and eventually President of the Continental Congress. More relevant is his importance in American Protestantism; he was a founder of the American Bible Society and the Society for Meliorating the Condition of the Jews, the goal of which was to evangelize and convert the Jews. Boudinot saw the American Revolution as a precursor to the coming millennium; and in the Jewish Indian theory he linked the roles of the American Indians and the United States itself as central to the return of the Christian messiah. His colleague, Thomas Jefferson, famously rejected Boudinot's views on this matter after consulting with John Adams.

cat. 50

Mordecai M. Noah (1785–1851)
Discourse on the Evidences of the American Indians Being the Descendants of the Lost Tribes of Israel. Delivered before the Mercantile Library Association, Clinton Hall
New York: James Van Norden, 1837

Mordecai M. Noah was the first nationally prominent Jewish figure in the United States; he was an author and newspaper editor active in the political life of the Jacksonian era. In this *Discourse* he reviewed and accepted the traditional linguistic, cultural, and religious arguments that the Indians were descendants

of the lost tribes. But Noah was also a utopian who had already proposed that a Jewish refuge be established on Grand Island, in the Niagara River near Buffalo, New York. That, however, was a failure.

Notes

1. Richard H. Popkin, "The Rise and Fall of the Jewish Indian Theory," in Yoseph Kaplan, Henry Mechoulan, and Richard H. Popkin, eds., *Menasseh ben Israel and His World* (Leiden: Brill, 1989), 63.
2. Zvi Ben-Dor Benite, *The Ten Lost Tribes: A World History* (New York: Oxford University Press, 2009), 215–19.
3. Jonathan Sarna, "Port Jews in the Atlantic: Further Thoughts," *Jewish History* 20 (2006): 215.

The Pennſylvania Packet, *and Daily Advertiſer.*

[Price Four-Pence.] WEDNESDAY, SEPTEMBER 19, 1787. EMMET COLL. DIV. NYPL [No. 2690.

WE, the People of the United States, in order to for a more perfect Union, eſtabliſh juſtice, inſure domeſ Tranquility, provide for the common Defence, pr mote the General Welfare, and ſecure the Bleſſings Liberty to Ourſelves and our Poſterity, do ordain and eſtabliſh th Conſtitution for the United States of America.

ARTICLE I.

Sect. 1. ALL legiſlative powers herein granted ſhall be veſted in a Congreſs of the United States, which ſhall conſiſt of a Senate and Houſe of Repreſentatives.

Sect. 2. The Houſe of Repreſentatives ſhall be compoſed of members choſen every ſecond year by the people of the ſeveral ſtates, and the electors in each ſtate ſhall have the qualifications requiſite for electors of the moſt numerous branch of the ſtate legiſlature.

No perſon ſhall be a repreſentative who ſhall not have attained to the age of twenty-five years, and been ſeven years a citizen of the United States, and who ſhall not, when elected, be an inhabitant of that ſtate in which he ſhall be choſen.

Repreſentatives and direct taxes ſhall be apportioned among the ſeveral ſtates which may be included within this Union, according to their reſpective numbers, which ſhall be determined by adding to the whole number of free perſons, including thoſe bound to ſervice for a term of years, and excluding Indians not taxed, three-fifths of all other perſons. The actual enumeration ſhall be made within three years after the firſt meeting of the Congreſs of the United States, and within every ſubſequent term of ten years, in ſuch manner as they ſhall by law direct. The number of repreſentatives ſhall not exceed one for every thirty thouſand, but each ſtate ſhall have at leaſt one repreſentative; and until ſuch enumeration ſhall be made, the ſtate of New-Hampſhire ſhall be entitled to chuſe three, Maſſachuſetts eight, Rhode-Iſland and Providence Plantations one, Connecticut five, New-York ſix, New-Jerſey four, Pennſylvania eight, Delaware one, Maryland ſix, Virginia ten, North-Carolina five, South-Carolina five, and Georgia three.

When vacancies happen in the repreſentation from any ſtate, the Executive authority thereof ſhall iſſue writs of election to fill ſuch vacancies.

The Houſe of Repreſentatives ſhall chuſe their Speaker and other officers; and ſhall have the ſole power of impeachment.

Sect. 3. The Senate of the United States ſhall be compoſed of two ſenators from each ſtate, choſen by the legiſlature thereof, for ſix years; and each ſenator ſhall have one vote.

5

Communities and Constitutions in Colonial North America

While the Jewish community of the English North American colonies numbered only a fraction of one percent of the total population, there were signs of continuity and novelty. For example, refugee New Christians still came from Portugal. But as communities grew in New York, Newport, Philadelphia, Charleston, and Savannah, the use of English spread while that of Hebrew and Spanish diminished. This marked the beginning of profound changes in how Jews in America (and the future United States) would choose an identity—or identities. Late in the eighteenth century, the American Revolution disrupted and divided Jewish communities. But it also led to the writing of critically important documents guaranteeing, or in some cases at least proposing, religious freedom for all faiths in the new Republic and its constituent states.

Religious life and learning remained defining features of Jewish life, though great changes were in store in the American environment. There is no question that Jews in the North American colonies exhibited an immensely full range of religiosity, adherence to traditional practices, and knowledge of Judaism (or lack thereof). The great American Jewish historian Jacob Rader Marcus referred to the "Jewish spectrum" prevailing from the second half of the eighteenth century to the first half of the nineteenth. "There was no end to the assortment of Jews who were to appear on the scene between 1776 and 1840: one sometimes wonders if there was such a thing as a typical Jew." Further, "The 'typical' American-born Jew was a religionist sui generis; he visited the synagog occasionally, associated primarily with Jews, kept the Sabbath after a fashion, and made a stab at maintaining a kosher home.... It is not easy to divide Jews into categories according to the degree of Orthodoxy or lack of it. Actually there were almost as many Judaisms as there were individuals."[1]

The first item included in this section is, however, a secular work, one that informed European Jews about scientific progress and also provided information about the New World. *Work of Toviyah* (1707–8) (cat. 51) indicates the New World with a diagram of a ship on the globe. The second item, concerning a complicated court case that was drawn out for almost a decade, illustrates the role that Jews played in transatlantic trade (cat. 52). The several entries that follow remind us of the linguistic changes that were taking place among North American Jews; another refers to Gentiles, specifically Harvard students, learning or at least studying Hebrew (cat. 55). These include an Amsterdam-published *Machzor*, or High Holidays prayer book, in Spanish, which could have been used by many American Jews (cat. 53). There is also one of the earliest English-language Jewish prayer books, translated and published in 1766 because North American Jews not only were losing knowledge of Hebrew, but of Spanish as well (cat. 56). There is also a sermon, given in Newport by a visiting rabbi from Ottoman-ruled Palestine, printed and translated into English for the same reasons (cat. 57). As the eighteenth century continued, with wars between the Atlantic powers and growing estrangement between Britain and its North American colonies, Jews responded to the eventual upsurge of revolutionary belief and action much the same as did their Christian neighbors. The community was divided, but there was nonetheless significant support for independence from Britain among Jews—at least in part because most American Jews had no connection of ancestry or background with that country.

Among The New York Public Library's strongest collections is that documenting the laws and constitutions of the revolutionary era and its immediate aftermath. It is necessary to return to the seventeenth century, however, and the great philosopher John Locke's *Fundamental Constitutions of Carolina*, written for that colony (cat. 59). Locke's statements insist on religious toleration for any "church" having at least seven members, including for Jews. William Penn's constitution for his "Province of Pennsilvania" (cat. 60) of 1682 similarly calls for general tolerance among all religious groups.

At the time of the revolution and immediately after, individual states composed and published their own constitutions. Two of the most important cases were New York and Virginia. New York allowed all men, including Jews, full political rights, as reflected in the state's constitution of 1777 (cat. 63). The 1776 Virginia Declaration of Rights, regarded as a model for the federal Bill of Rights, provided for free exercise of religion, and Thomas Jefferson followed it with "An Act for Establishing Religious Freedom." The United States Constitution of 1787 and the Bill of Rights (1791) mandated freedom of religious practice and rejected any religious test for offices, but these mandates then referred only to Congress and the federal government, and not to individual states (cat. 64). In the same year, the *Ordinance* for the newly established Northwest Territory rejected any religious tests or restrictions (cat. 65). Through the end of the eighteenth century and much of the nineteenth, all the states eliminated restrictions on religious freedom and political and civil rights for Jews as well as Catholics, Protestant dissenters, and ultimately all religious groups and even non-religious individuals (albeit within the usual confines of American racial laws).

This chapter concludes with a few documents relating to Aaron Lopez, one of the greatest Jewish merchants of the colonies (cat. 66–68). Coming to America in the 1750s, Lopez, of Newport, Rhode Island, made his fortune in whale oil, widely used to make candles. The documents refer to transactions with the Vernon brothers of Newport, who were among the most important figures in the African slave trade. Lopez and his partner, Jacob Rodriguez Rivera, traded in slaves as well, if on a modest scale.[2] This reminds us that the Jews, in secular respects, took on the values and behavior of the Christian majority of the American colonies; and also that the economies and societies of the New World were, to a large degree, built on chattel slavery.

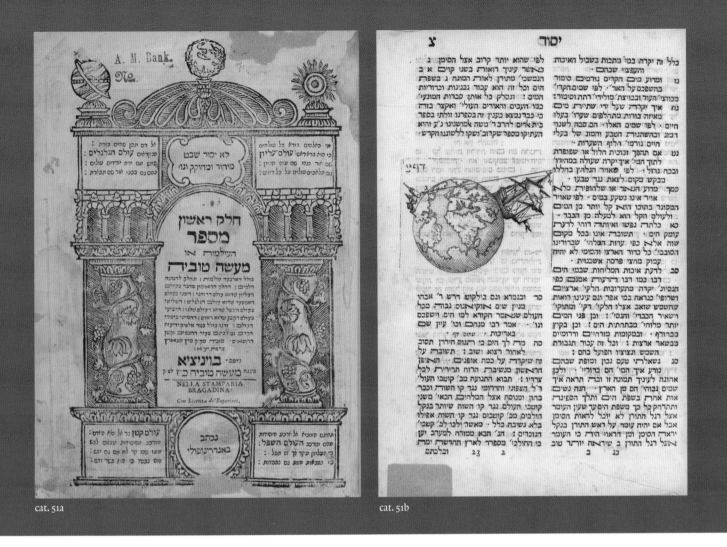

cat. 51a

cat. 51b

cat. 51

Toviyah Kats (1652?–1729)

מעשה טוביה

Maaseh Toviyah (Work of Toviyah)

Venice: Bragadin, 1707–8

Page: Title page

Page: A ship travels the globe, on which are delineated both Europe and the New World

The author, who was born in Metz, France, wrote this book while in Adrianople (now Edirne), in the Ottoman Empire. He was a physician first in Poland, then served in the courts of several Ottoman Sultans. An early scientific reference work in Hebrew, it presents the current knowledge prevailing in many branches of science, including geography (with a map of the world showing Europe and America). It is from this book that Jews in Central and East European countries, who typically received little or no secular education, first became acquainted with discoveries in modern science. Thus, as the Ashkenazic and Central and East European tide of Jewish immigration to the New World grew throughout the eighteenth and early nineteenth centuries, it is not unlikely that this book was consulted frequently. It also appears to be the first work in Hebrew mentioning tobacco—so important to the Atlantic economy—and its supposed medicinal properties.

cat. 52

New York Court of Chancery

The Decree in the Case of Solomon De Medina, Mosesson and Company, Merchants in London …

New York: Printed and sold by W. Bradford, 1728

Page: Title page

Sir Solomon de Medina (ca. 1650–1730), a military contractor, ranked among the most prominent Jews in England and was the first to be knighted. This volume illustrates Jews' roles in the tangles of international trade. It concerns an extraordinarily complex court case that took nine years to settle: the disputed ownership of a large shipment of tobacco stored in New York, against the backdrop of conflicts among three European states (Spain, France, and Britain). An English privateer "took, and brought into the Port of *New-York*, the Ship *Victory, belonging to the India Company of France* … having on board … 2217 Bags of *Tobacco* in Snuff, and sundry quantities of *Tobacco* in Rolls & Hands, great part whereof had been loaded at the *Havana* for the King of *Spain*, then an Enemy, to be delivered at *Cadiz* in *Spain*, on payment of 13000 Pieces of Eight, Freight." This was in the "5th year of King *George* [I]," that is, 1719 (p. 1).

But the Court of Admiralty in New York found that the King of Spain had sold the cargo to de Medina before the capture, and the privateer's claim was disallowed. While the case was appealed to London, the court ordered the tobacco to be stored in the warehouse of Rene Het (or Hett) and Andrew Fresneau in New York.

The court's decision was upheld, and de Medina's agents tried take possession of the tobacco; but then Het and Fresneau's heirs (he had died) presented them with extraordinarily large invoices, in all almost £3,000. Even then de Medina's agents found that much of the tobacco was missing. Eventually it was learned that some of the tobacco had been sold by Het, and that some had been hidden "in private Places" (p. 6). By this time Het had "absconded" (p. 12).

The compiler of this volume summed up the case thusly: "so great a number of *Frauds, Perjuries* and *foul-Dealings* do Evidently appear in this case, beside what further may be presumed; and so great a number of *Contrivances* of *Delay* and *Vexation* to the Complainants [de Medina and his representatives], in the Course of this Suit, to hinder the coming at Justice, that the like of both, has not in any one case, in all Probability, ever appeared" (p. 32). The book concludes, "Great is Truth, and it will Prevail" (appendix, p. 4). Besides the inherent fascination with the case's complications, it is significant because of the Jewish involvement in an American colonial court case that dealt with the ownership of quantities of an American product kept in a New York warehouse, against the backdrop of the conflicts among the great Atlantic powers of the day— Spain, France, and England.

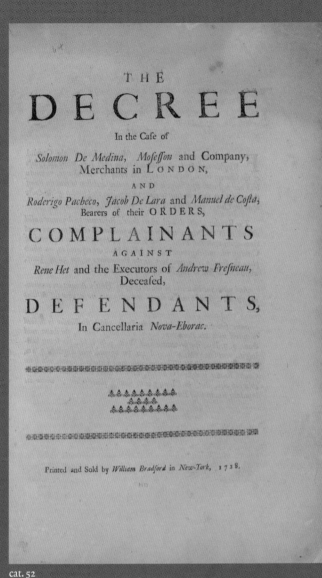

THE
DECREE

In the Cafe of

Solomon De Medina, Mofeſſon and Company,
Merchants in LONDON,

AND

Roderigo Pacheco, Jacob De Lara and Manuel de Coſta,
Bearers of their ORDERS,

COMPLAINANTS

AGAINST

Rene Het and the Executors of Andrew Freſneau,
Deceaſed,

DEFENDANTS,

In Cancellaria Nova-Eborac.

Printed and Sold by William Bradford in New-York, 1728.

cat. 52

ORDEN
DE
ROS-ASANAH
Y
KIPUR
Por eſtillo corriente y ſegui-
do ſin bolver de una aotra
Parte, como ſe uza en eſte
Kahal Kados de
AMSTERDAM,
Acoſta de
AHARON HISQUIA QUERIDO

ANNO
5486

cat. 53

cat. 53

Orden de Ros-Asanah y Kipur por estillo corriente y seguido sin bolver de una aotra parte, como se uza en este Kahal Kados de Amsterdam (The order of service for Rosh-Hashanah and Yom Kippur, in current style and followed without turning from one part to another, according to the usage of this Kahal Kadosh of Amsterdam)
Amsterdam: Aharon Hisquia Querido, 5486 [1726]
Page: Title page

This early edition of the *Machzor* (High Holidays liturgy), published in Amsterdam and translated into Spanish, would have been used by Jews of Spanish or Portuguese origin in the Americas.

cat. 54

Bernard Picart (1673–1733)
Cérémonies et coutumes religieuses de tous les peuples du monde
(Ceremonies and religious costumes of all the world's peoples)
Amsterdam: J. Bernard, 1723–37
Page: Illustration from volume 1, following page 100

Bernard Picart was a French Protestant who settled in Amsterdam. Many of his drawings of Jewish religious practices were drawn from life in the city's great Portuguese synagogue. In this illustration, Picart recreates the synagogue's 1675 dedication. The main synagogue of Amsterdam was the parent of all Dutch Portuguese synagogues in the New World in the colonial period.

A. *l'Hechal où on garde les livres de la Loy.*
B. *Thebá ou Pupître où le Hazan et Hacham lisent la Li*
C. *Les 2 Galeries pour les femmes.*

cat. 54

A DEDICACE DE LA SYNAGOGUE DES JUIFS PORTUGAIS, A AMSTERDAM.

B. Picart delineavit et sculp. direx. 1721

La dedicace de la Synagogue et l'entrée des livres de la Loy, se celebra
pendant 8. jours, le 10.e du mois de Menahem 5435, qui se raporte au
mois d'Aout 1675, on en fait la commemoration tous les Ans.

cat. 55

Judah Monis (1683–1764)

דקדוק לשון עברית

Dickdook Leshon Gnebreet [Dikduk leshon Ivrit]. A Grammar of the Hebrew Tongue, Being an Essay to Bring the Hebrew Grammar into English

Boston: Printed by Jonas Green, MDCCXXXV [1735]

Judah Monis, from a converso family that had returned to Judaism, was born and educated in Europe. He immigrated to New York, then to Massachusetts. At the time, Harvard College had a Hebrew instruction requirement, and Monis, by his command of the language, was qualified to teach it— except that all Harvard instructors had to be Christians. He studied with Protestant ministers and converted in 1722, and was then quickly hired to teach at Harvard. In the same year he published a book with this unsubtle title: *The Truth, Being a Discourse Which the Author Delivered at His Baptism, Containing Nine Principal Arguments the Modern Jewish Rabbins Do Make to Prove, the Messiah Is Yet to Come: with the Answers to Each, Not Only According to the Orthodox Opinion, But Even with the Authority of Their Own Authentick Rabbins of Old.* The preface was by the Puritan minister Increase Mather (1639–1723). Regardless, his was a controversial case; critics claimed it was an insincere, opportunistic conversion. Monis's Hebrew grammar textbook was published thirteen years after his conversion and hiring by Harvard. The first two letters of the transliteration *gnebreet* (which means "Hebrew") in the title are not errors. They are an attempt to represent the Hebrew guttural consonant *ayin*.

cat. 56

Isaac Pinto (1720–1791)

Prayers for Shabbath, Rosh-Hashanah, and Kippur, or, the Sabbath, the Beginning of the Year, and the Day of Atonements: with the Amidah and Musaph of the Moadim, or Solemn Seasons, According to the Order of the Spanish and Portuguese Jews

New York: Printed by John Holt, A.M. 5526 [1766]

Page: [94], "Morning Service of Kippur"

This early English translation of a Hebrew prayer book— one of the first—was printed in British Colonial New York, surprisingly, rather than in London, which had the larger and wealthier English-speaking Jewish community. (A 1761 New York-printed translation, not in the Library's collections, appeared anonymously and without a prefatory explanation.) The translator of this volume, Isaac Pinto, a member of New York's Sephardic Congregation Shearith Israel, explained the reason for the English edition in his introduction. His comments are telling with regard to the religious needs and linguistic changes then going on among New York's Jews, as well as elsewhere in the North American colonies:

A Veneration for the Language, sacred by being that in which it pleased Almighty God to reveal himself to our Ancestors, and a desire to preserve it, in firm Persuasion that it will again be re-established in Israel; are probably leading Reasons for our performing divine Service in Hebrew: But that, being imperfectly understood by many, by some, not at all; it has been necessary to translate our Prayers, in the Language of the Country wherein it

MORNING SERVICE
OF
KIPPUR.

On the Morning of Kippur, *before* Nifhmath col *Hai, fay this* Petition of Ribbi Yehudah Ha Levy.

Adonai negdecha col Taavati.

O LORD, thou knoweft my whole Defire, although I with my Lips, do not exprefs it: I humbly requeft thy Favour a Moment, if I *then* expire: And Oh that my Requeft were granted: I would commend my remaining Spirit into thine Hand; then go to Reft, and pleafing to me, would be my Sleep.

When I depart from thee, I find Death, while I yet live; and if unto thee I adhere, even in my Death, I have Life. But alas! I know not what Offering I fhall bring, and how I fhall worfhip, or what my Duty. Teach me, O LORD, thy Ways, and deliver me from the Bondage and Captivity of my Folly. Inftruct me while I am able to humble myfelf *before thee*, and defpife not my Affliction; before the Day *cometh*, in which I fhall be a Burthen unto myfelf; and when one Part of me becometh a Weight unto the other: *Even before* I be depreffed with old Age, and my Bones become corroded, that they be weary of fupporting me; and that I remove to the Place where my Fathers have gone; and retire to Repofe, in the Place of their Reft. I am in this World as a Sojourn-

65

cat. 56

hath pleafed the divine Providence to appoint our Lot. In Europe, the Spanish and Portuguese Jews have a Translation in Spanish, which as they generally understand, may be sufficient; but that not being the Case in the British Dominions in America, has induced me to Attempt a Translation in English, not without Hope that it will tend to the Improvement of many of my Brethren in their Devotion.

fig. 11
"Ezra Stiles S.T.D.
L.L.D. President of
Yale College," stipple
engraving drawn and
engraved by Samuel Hill,
Boston, ca. 1789–95

fig. 12
Color postcard of the
"Interior of the Oldest Jewish
Synagogue in the Country.
Newport, R.I." (Providence:
The Rhode Island News
Company, ca. 1895–1907)

fig. 11

cat. 57

Haijm Isaac Karigal (1733–1777)
*A Sermon Preached at the Synagogue, in Newport, Rhode-Island,
called "The Salvation of Israel": On the day of Pentecost, or Feast of
weeks, the 6th day of the month Sivan, the year of the creation,
5533; or, May 28, 1773. Being the anniversary of giving the law at
Mount Sinai: by the venerable Hocham, the learned Rabbi, Haijm
Isaac Karigal …*
Newport: Printed and sold by S. Southwick, 1773

Karigal (or Carigal) was born in Hebron, in Ottoman-ruled
Palestine, and traveled through much of the Mediterranean world and Europe, plus Curaçao, Jamaica, and, in
1772 and 1773, Philadelphia, New York, and Newport. He
subsequently served as a rabbi in Barbados. Besides this
sermon, originally given in Spanish (or Ladino) on the
holiday of Shavuot, he is known in American history
through the writings of Connecticut minister and Yale
College president Ezra Stiles (1727–1795), who befriended
him on his visit to Newport. Through Stiles, Karigal had a
significant if indirect influence on Yale's development.
Stiles strongly believed that his students should study the
Bible in the original, and he himself was tutored by Karigal
and corresponded with him in Hebrew. Stiles even
commissioned a portrait of Karigal for Yale. *Hocham*, used
in the sermon's title, is a variant transliterated spelling of
Haham, "wise man" or "sage," the Hebrew term traditionally used by Sephardim for rabbis. This translation
demonstrates that, significantly, North American-born
Jews increasingly preferred English to Spanish.[4]

fig. 12

cat. 58

Joshua Hezekiah DeCordova (1720–1797)

אמת ואמונה

*Emet ve-emunah. Reason and Faith, or, Philosophical
Absurdities, and the Necessity of Revelation. Intended to
Promote Faith among Infidels, and the Unbounded Exercise of
Humanity among All Religious Men. By One of the Sons of
Abraham to His Brethren*

Philadelphia: F. Bailey, 1791

DeCordova served in his native Amsterdam and Curaçao
before he was appointed rabbi of the Jewish community
in Jamaica, a position he retained until his death. His
Reason and Faith is a defense of traditional faith against
"modern philosophers who destroy all principles of
faith and virtue." A polemic directed against deists and
freethinkers, the work, published first in Jamaica, was
reprinted in Philadelphia. The first line of Hebrew on
the title page means "Truth [or Reason] and Faith." The
second line, at the bottom, is an ancient rabbinic
instruction: "Da Ma she-Tashiv la-Apikorus" (Know
what you will respond to the heretic), from *Pirke avot*
(Sayings of the Fathers), 2:14. Its point is that one should
arm oneself with sufficient knowledge to combat those
who deny traditional religion. It is of interest that the
Hebrew term *Apikorus* (heretic) derives from the Greek
Epikouros, after the founder (d. 270 BCE) of the
philosophy of Epicureanism.

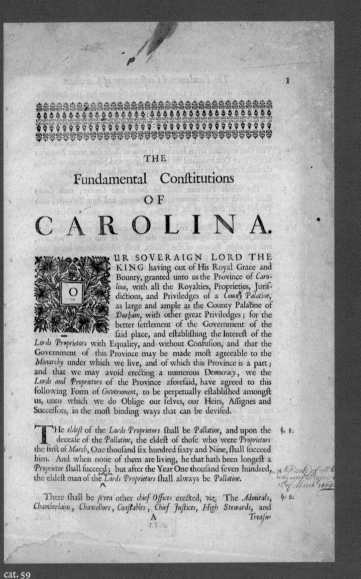

cat. 59

cat. 59

John Locke (1632–1704)

The Fundamental Constitutions of Carolina

London, 1670

Page: 1

The writings of John Locke, the champion of individual liberty, ranked high among the later Founding Fathers' intellectual inspirations. He was asked to help write the Carolina province's constitution. Carolina was one of several privately or shareholder-owned colonies, and included present-day North and South Carolina. Completed in 1669 but never fully ratified, the *Constitutions* promoted religious toleration, partly to ensure "*Civil Peace* . . . amidst the diversity of Opinions," but furthermore, so that "*Jews, Heathens*, and other *Dissenters* from the purity of *Christian Religion*, may not be scared and kept at a distance from it, but by having an opportunity of acquainting themselves with the truth and reasonableness of its *Doctrines,* and the peaceableness and inoffensiveness of its *Professors*, may by *good usage* and *persuasion* . . . be won over to embrace, and unfeignedly receive the *Truth*; Therefore any seven, or more Persons agreeing in any *Religion*, shall Constitute a *Church* or *Profession*, to which they shall give some Name, to distinguish it from others" (p. 21).

But even without regard to Locke's hope of conversion of Jews, heathens, and Christian dissenters, this is not a call for full toleration or acceptance of, for example, atheism. Locke states that no one can be a "*Freeman* of *Carolina*," or have an "Estate or Habitation" in the province without acknowledging that there is a God, and an afterlife of "happiness or misery." Further, he states that every "*Church* or *Profession*" must accept that God exists and is "publickly to be Worshipped," and that it must be possible for its members to "witness a Truth" by "laying Hands on, or kissing the Bible, as in the Church of England, *or by holding up the Hand, or any other sensible way*" (pp. 20–22). Regardless, Locke's statements here and elsewhere represent critical steps toward general toleration and freedom of religious belief and practice without the burden of established churches.

The New York Public Library's copy has marginal notes, some probably in Locke's own hand.

cat. 60

William Penn (1644–1718)

The Frame of the Government of Pennsilvania in America

[London: Printed by William Bradford], 1682

Page: 1

We have already seen that William Penn accepted the
notion that American Indians were Jews—partly on the
basis of their alleged physical resemblance to Jews, who
had started to arrive in London in the late 1650s, after
Manasseh ben Israel's mission (see cat. 45). Penn became
a leading figure in the newly founded Society of Friends,
or Quakers, as a young man in the 1660s. In the late
1670s he participated in the establishment of Quaker
communities in what is now New Jersey. In 1681 King
Charles II made a massive land grant to Penn, across the
Delaware River; this became, of course, Pennsylvania.
The next year Penn, pursuing his Quaker principles,
composed this *Frame of the Government*, which, like
Locke's document above, featured significant plans for
religious tolerance. Article 35 states: "That all persons
living in this Province, who confess and acknowledge
the One Almighty and Eternal God, to be the Creator,
Upholder and Ruler of the World, and that hold
themselves obliged in Conscience to live peaceably and
justly in *Civil Society*, shall in no wayes be molested or
prejudiced for their Religious Persuasion or Practice in
matters of *Faith* and *Worship*, nor shall they be compelled
at any time to frequent or maintain any Religious
Worship, Place or Ministry whatever." The previous

cat. 60

article, however, required that all officials and elected
members of the elected council or assembly must "profess
Faith in Jesus Christ" (pp. 10–11).

cat. 61

In Convention. June 12, 1776. A Declaration of Rights Made by the Representatives of the Good People of Virginia, Assembled in Full and Free Convention; Which Rights Do Pertain to Them, and Their Posterity, as the Basis and Foundation of Government
[Williamsburg, Va., 1776]

The Virginia Declaration of Rights of 1776 was largely written by George Mason and served as a model for the United States Constitution's Bill of Rights. See article XVI: "That religion, or the duty which we owe to our Creator, and the manner of discharging it, can be directed only by reason and conviction, not by force or violence; and therefore, all men are equally entitled to the free exercise of religion, according to the dictates of conscience; and that it is the mutual duty of all to practice Christian forbearance, love, and charity, towards each other" (p. [2]). The reference to "Christian" virtues is not, in fact, sectarian; it is a normal usage of the time, with ethical rather than specifically religious overtones.

cat. 62

Thomas Jefferson (1743–1826)
Notes on the State of Virginia
[Paris], 1782 [1785–6?]

Jefferson's book was written "for the use of a Foreigner of distinction, in answer to certain queries proposed by him." Appended to some copies of the *Notes* (including two of the three copies held by The New York Public Library) is Jefferson's "An Act for Establishing Religious Freedom, passed in the Assembly of Virginia in the beginning of the year 1786" (1786). This publication does not specifically mention Jews, but like the Virginia Declaration of Rights, it is extraordinarily significant in the history of American religious freedom. One of the Library's copies is a presentation copy to "Mr. Rittenhouse from Th. Jefferson."

cat. 63

The Constitution of the State of New-York
Philadelphia: Printed and sold by Styner and Cist, 1777
Page: 31, Article XXXVIII

When the Declaration of Independence held it self-evident that all men are created equal, endowed by their Creator with certain inalienable rights, it provided a degree of equality for Jews that had never existed in a modern nation. New York's first state constitution, drafted in the summer of 1776 by John Jay and adopted on April 20, 1777, by the Constitutional Convention in Kingston, New York, was very clear on this matter. Article 38 states: "This Convention doth further, in the name and by the authority of the good people of this State, Ordain, Determine and Declare, that the free exercise and enjoyment of religious profession and worship, without discrimination or preference, shall for ever hereafter be allowed within this State to all mankind."

cat. 64

The Constitution of the United States of America. Agreed to in Convention, at Philadelphia, September 17, 1787
Trenton: Printed and sold by Isaac Collins, M.DCC.LXXXVII [1787]
Page: Front page of *The Pennsylvania Packet, and Daily Advertiser*, which devoted its entire issue of September 19, 1787, to a printing of the newly drawn Constitution of the United States

Article 6 states unequivocally: "The senators and representatives...and all executive and judicial officers, both of the United States and of the several States, shall be bound by oath or affirmation, to support this constitution; but no religious test shall ever be required as a qualification to any office or publick trust under the United States." The First Amendment of the Bill of Rights (that is, the first ten amendments to the Constitution), states: "Congress shall make no law respecting an establishment of religion, or prohibiting the free exercise thereof; or abridging the freedom of speech, or of the press; or the right of the people peaceably to assemble, and to petition the Government for a redress of grievances." It must be noted, however, that only Congress, and not the individual states, was originally bound by the establishment and free exercise clauses, though similar ideas appeared in some state constitutions. The original Articles of Confederation, drafted in 1777 and adopted in 1781, do not refer to the topic of religion, but this is to be expected since the document does not concern itself with matters of individual behavior or belief.

cat. 65

An Ordinance for the Government of the Territory of the United States, North-West of the River Ohio
[New York: Francis Childs and John Swaine for John Dunlap of Philadelphia, 1787]

The establishment of the Northwest Territory, covering the eventual five states of Ohio, Indiana, Illinois, Michigan, and Wisconsin, was one of the most important acts of the Confederation Congress. Among other critical elements, the 1787 *Ordinance* proclaimed civil liberties and banned slavery in the new territory, and said that the "utmost good faith shall always be observed towards the Indians." With regard to religious beliefs and practices, Article 1 states with certainty: "No person, demeaning himself in a peaceable and orderly manner, shall ever be molested on account of his mode of worship or religious sentiments in the said territory."

cat. 66–68

Aaron Lopez (1731–1782)
Business records, Newport, Rhode Island

Jacob Rodriguez Rivera to William Vernon
Invoice for spermaceti candles, February 24, 1754

Aaron Lopez to Samuel and William Vernon
Invoice for spermaceti candles, December 24, 1767

Aaron Lopez to Samuel and William Vernon
Invoice for spermaceti candles, March 21, 1768

(31)

their lands, have in divers instances been productive of dangerous discontents and animosities: BE IT ORDAINED, that no purchases or contracts for the sale of lands made since the fourteenth day of October, in the year of our Lord, one thousand seven hundred and seventy-five, or which may hereafter be made with or of the said Indians, within the limits of this State, shall be binding on the said Indians, or deemed valid, unless made under the authority, and with the consent of the legislature of this State.

XXXVIII. AND WHEREAS we are required by the benevolent principles of rational liberty, not only to expel civil tyranny, but also to guard against that spiritual oppression and intolerance, wherewith the bigotry and ambition of weak and wicked priests and princes, have scourged mankind : This Convention doth further, in the name and by the authority of the good people of this State, ORDAIN, DETERMINE and DECLARE, that the free exercise and enjoyment of religious profession and worship, without discrimination or preference, shall for ever hereafter be allowed within this State to all mankind. Provided that the liberty of conscience hereby granted, shall not be so construed, as to excuse acts of licentiousness, or justify practices inconsistent with the peace or safety of this State.

XXXIX. AND WHEREAS the ministers of the gospel, are by their profession dedicated to the service of God and the cure of souls, and ought not to be diverted from the great duties of their

cat. 63

The Pennsylvania Packet, and Daily Advertiser.

[Price Four-Pence.]   WEDNESDAY, September 19, 1787.   [No. 2690.]

WE, the People of the United States, in order to form a more perfect Union, establish justice, insure domestic Tranquility, provide for the common Defence, promote the General Welfare, and secure the Blessings of Liberty to Ourselves and our Posterity, do ordain and establish this Constitution for the United States of America.

ARTICLE I.

Sect. 1. ALL legislative powers herein granted shall be vested in a Congress of the United States, which shall consist of a Senate and House of Representatives.

Sect. 2. The House of Representatives shall be composed of members chosen every second year by the people of the several states, and the electors in each state shall have the qualifications requisite for electors of the most numerous branch of the state legislature.

No person shall be a representative who shall not have attained to the age of twenty-five years, and been seven years a citizen of the United States, and who shall not, when elected, be an inhabitant of that state in which he shall be chosen.

Representatives and direct taxes shall be apportioned among the several states which may be included within this Union, according to their respective numbers, which shall be determined by adding to the whole number of free persons, including those bound to service for a term of years, and excluding Indians not taxed, three-fifths of all other persons. The actual enumeration shall be made within three years after the first meeting of the Congress of the United States, and within every subsequent term of ten years, in such manner as they shall by law direct. The number of representatives shall not exceed one for every thirty thousand, but each state shall have at least one representative; and until such enumeration shall be made, the state of New-Hampshire shall be entitled to chuse three, Massachusetts eight, Rhode-Island and Providence Plantations one, Connecticut five, New-York six, New-Jersey four, Pennsylvania eight, Delaware one, Maryland six, Virginia ten, North-Carolina five, South-Carolina five, and Georgia three.

When vacancies happen in the representation from any state, the Executive authority thereof shall issue writs of election to fill such vacancies.

The House of Representatives shall chuse their Speaker and other officers; and shall have the sole power of impeachment.

Sect. 3. The Senate of the United States shall be composed of two senators from each state, chosen by the legislature thereof, for six years; and each senator shall have one vote.

Immediately after they shall be assembled in consequence of the first election, they shall be divided as equally as may be into three classes. The seats of the senators of the first class shall be vacated at the expiration of the second year, of the second class at the expiration of the fourth year, and of the third class at the expiration of the sixth year, so that one-third may be chosen every second year; and if vacancies happen by resignation, or otherwise, during the recess of the Legislature of any state, the Executive thereof may make temporary appointments until the next meeting of the Legislature, which shall then fill such vacancies.

No person shall be a senator who shall not have attained to the age of thirty years, and been nine years a citizen of the United States, and who shall not, when elected, be an inhabitant of that state for which he shall be chosen.

The Vice-President of the United States shall be President of the senate, but shall have no vote, unless they be equally divided.

The Senate shall chuse their other officers, and also a President pro tempore, in the absence of the Vice-President, or when he shall exercise the office of President of the United States.

The Senate shall have the sole power to try all impeachments. When sitting for that purpose, they shall be on oath or affirmation. When the President of the United States is tried, the Chief Justice shall preside: And no person shall be convicted without the concurrence of two-thirds of the members present.

Judgment in cases of impeachment shall not extend further than to removal from office, and disqualification to hold and enjoy any office of honor, trust or profit under the United States; but the party convicted shall nevertheless be liable and subject to indictment, trial, judgment and punishment, according to law.

Sect. 4. The times, places and manner of holding elections for senators and representatives, shall be prescribed in each state by the legislature thereof; but the Congress may at any time by law make or alter such regulations, except as to the places of chusing Senators.

The Congress shall assemble at least once in every year, and such meeting shall be on the first Monday in December, unless they shall by law appoint a different day.

Sect. 5. Each house shall be the judge of the elections, returns and qualifications of its own members, and a majority of each shall constitute a quorum to do business; but a smaller number may adjourn from day to day, and may be authorised to compel the attendance of absent members, in such manner, and under such penalties as each house may provide.

Each house may determine the rules of its proceedings, punish its members for disorderly behaviour, and, with the concurrence of two-thirds, expel a member.

Each house shall keep a journal of its proceedings, and from time to time publish the same, excepting such parts as may in their judgment require secrecy; and the yeas and nays of the members of either house on any question shall, at the desire of one-fifth of those present, be entered on the journal.

Neither house, during the session of Congress, shall, without the consent of the other, adjourn for more than three days, nor to any other place than that in which the two houses shall be sitting.

Sect. 6. The senators and representatives shall receive a compensation for their services, to be ascertained by law, and paid out of the treasury of the United States. They shall in all cases, except treason, felony and breach of the peace, be privileged from arrest during their attendance at the session of their respective houses, and in going to and returning from the same; and for any speech or debate in either house, they shall not be questioned in any other place.

No senator or representative shall, during the time for which he was elected, be appointed to any civil office under the authority of the United States, which shall have been created, or the emoluments whereof shall have been encreased during such time; and no person holding any office under the United States, shall be a member of either house during his continuance in office.

Sect. 7. All bills for raising revenue shall originate in the house of representatives; but the senate may propose or concur with amendments as on other bills.

Every bill which shall have passed the house of representatives and the senate, shall, before it become a law, be presented to the president of the United States; if he approve he shall sign it, but if not he shall return it, with his objections to that house in which it shall have originated, who shall enter the objections at large on their journal, and proceed to reconsider it. If after such reconsideration two-thirds of that house shall agree to pass the bill, it shall be sent, together with the objections, to the other house, by which it shall likewise be reconsidered, and if approved by two-thirds of that house, it shall become a law. But in all such cases the votes of both houses shall

cat. 64

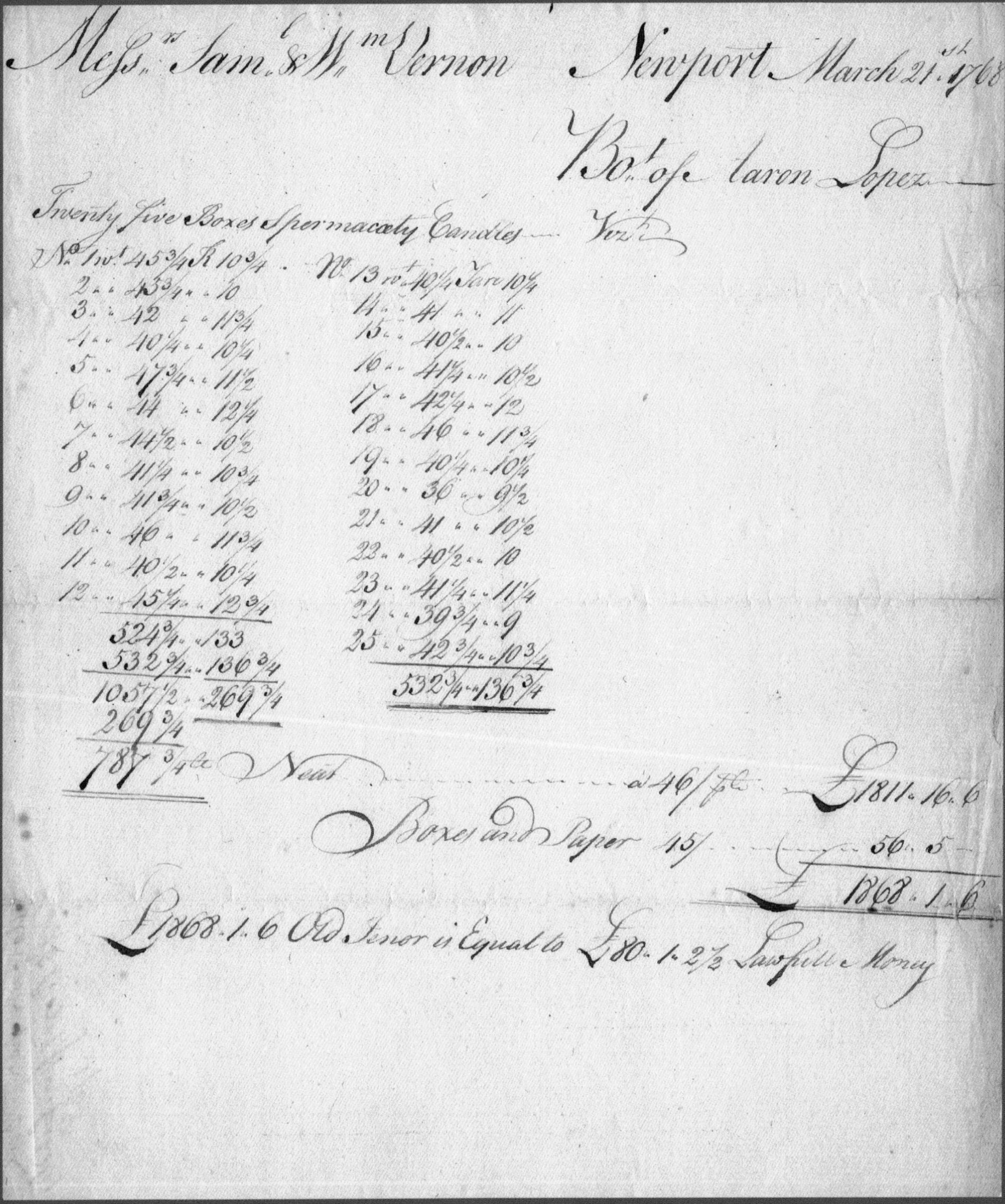

Mess.rs Sam.l & Wm Vernon Newport March 21st 1768

Bo.t of Aaron Lopez ——

Twenty five Boxes Spermacaety Candles —— Viz.t

No.	w.t	T.r	No.	w.t	Tare
1	45¾	10¾	13	40¼	10¼
2	45¾	10	14	41	11
3	42	11¾	15	40½	10
4	40¼	10¼	16	41¼	10½
5	47¾	11½	17	42¼	12
6	44	12¼	18	46	11¾
7	44½	10½	19	40¼	10¼
8	41¼	10¾	20	36	9½
9	41¾	10½	21	41	10½
10	46	11¾	22	40½	10
11	40½	10¼	23	41¼	11¼
12	45¼	12¾	24	39¾	9
	524¾	133	25	42¾	10¾
	532¾	136¾		532¾	136¾
	1057½	269¾			
	269¾				

787¾ lb Neat .... @ 46/ ₰ lb £1811.16.6

Boxes and Paper 45/ 56.5

£1868.1.6

£1868.1.6 Old Tenor is Equal to £80.1.2½ Lawfull Money

cat. 68

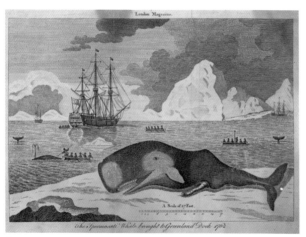

fig. 13

fig. 13
"The Spermacaeti Whale brought
to Greenland Dock 1762," etching
published in *The London Magazine,
or, Gentleman's Monthly Intelligencer,*
Vol. XXXI, February 1762

Aaron Lopez, one of the leading businessmen in the British North American colonies, emigrated from Portugal to the thriving port city of Newport, Rhode Island, where he adopted Judaism and the name Aaron. He had a thriving sperm whale-oil candle business with his father-in-law, Jacob Rodriguez Rivera (1717–1789), as senior partner. Lopez started the United Company of Spermaceti Chandlers, an association of manufacturers that negotiated prices with the Nantucket whalers and deterred competitors. Known as the Spermaceti Trust, the association was a model for later cartels. He was also a prominent philanthropist and one of the founders of Newport's synagogue, now the oldest surviving synagogue building in the U.S., known as the Touro Synagogue (see fig. 12). As an American patriot, he left Newport for Massachusetts when the British arrived in the port. He died in Leicester, Massachusetts, in 1782. At Lopez's death, Yale College president Ezra Stiles wrote in his diary: "a Merchant of the first Eminence; for Honor & Extent of Commerce probably surpassed by no Merch[ant] in America.... Without a single Enemy & the most universally beloved by an extensive Acquaintance of any man I ever Knew."[5]

The Vernon brothers—Samuel (1711–1792) and William (1719–1806)—of Newport were leading figures in the American slave trade. The Vernon family belonged to Newport's Second Congregational Church, of which Ezra Stiles was pastor for many years.

Notes

1. Jacob Rader Marcus, *United States Jewry, 1776–1985* (Detroit: Wayne State University Press, 1989–93), 1: 610, 612–13.

2. The involvement of Jews in the American slave trade is an important part of the larger matter of American slaveholding and race relations. On Lopez and his colleagues, an early article is Virginia Bever Platt, "'And Don't Forget the Guinea Voyage': The Slave Trade of Aaron Lopez of Newport," *William and Mary Quarterly* 32 (1975): 601–18. A more recent general work is Eli Faber, *Jews, Slaves, and the Slave Trade: Setting the Record Straight* (New York: New York University Press, 1998). Jonathan Schorsch, *Jews and Blacks in the Early Modern World* (Cambridge: Cambridge University Press, 2004), takes in an even broader scope.

4. Laura Liebman, "From Holy Land to New England Canaan: Rabbi Haim Carigal and Sephardic Itinerant Preaching in the Eighteenth Century," *Early American Literature* 44 (2009): 73.

5. Ezra Stiles, *Ezra Stiles and the Jews: Selected Passages from His Literary Diary Concerning Jews and Judaism*, with critical and explanatory notes by George Alexander Kohut (New York: P. Cowen, 1902), 138–39. A complex portrait of Stiles's attitudes can be found in Arthur A. Chiel, "Ezra Stiles and the Jews: A Study in Ambivalence," in *A Bicentennial Festschrift for Jacob Rader Marcus*, ed. Bertram Wallace Korn (Waltham, Mass.: American Jewish Historical Society; New York: Ktav, 1976), 63–76.

6

The Long Nineteenth Century of the Jews in America

Historians of Europe sometimes refer to the "long nineteenth century."[1] This is the idea that the century and a quarter from the French Revolution of 1789 to the First World War in 1914–18 can be usefully approached as a distinct and unified era in European history—in political, socioeconomic, and cultural terms, stretching between two cataclysms. And in any case, there is no question that dividing history by centuries, marching along by 100-year breaks, is rarely profitable, and distorts the historical understanding more than it enlightens.

Something similar can also be applied to the history of Jews in the new American confederation, and then republic. This "long nineteenth century" could be said to reach from the American Revolution's conclusion, a few years before the French Revolution ended that powerful and long-lasting monarchy; and then a little past the end of World War I, into the early 1920s. The reason for the slightly later conclusion, as compared to that of Europe's "long nineteenth century," is the fact that, beyond the negative impact of the war on immigration (large-scale migration picked up almost immediately after the war's end), in 1921 and 1924 stringent new laws were passed that radically cut immigration to America, including that of European Jews. Thus the early 1920s unquestionably represent a profound caesura in American Jewish history. Using the concept of the "long century" also reminds us of the importance of closely linking developments in the

countries of emigration (European states and empires) with developments in the United States and other countries in the Americas.

Significant numbers of Central European Jews arrived, especially from the 1820s to the 1860s, the decades leading up to the American Civil War (and through it and beyond). This has led to the commonly expressed idea that the early-middle decades of the nineteenth century were a kind of German era of Jewish immigration and settlement in the United States. It is true that Jews from the German states were among the largest and most important groups in these decades. But Jews from other states—among them France, Britain, and the Austro-Hungarian (Habsburg) empire—came in significant numbers as well. Some of these last were primarily German-speakers, of course, among them those who had received educations in the schools of, for example, Bohemia, Moravia, and Galicia, important constituent hereditary lands of the Habsburgs. Beginning in the 1870s, increasingly large numbers of Jewish immigrants came from Austria-Hungary (notably Austria proper, Bohemia, Galicia, and the transleithan territories under the Hungarian crown), the vast Russian empire, and from smaller states, such as Romania, Greece, and states that had emerged as a result of the decline of Ottoman Turkish rule in the Balkans. Significant numbers came from Turkey proper, as well.

The traditional and popular narrative of the Jews' coming to America has frequently set 1881–82 as a critically important break, dividing the chiefly German immigrant era before it from the largely Russian, Polish, and generally Eastern European era that is supposed to have followed. This is tied to the idea that increasing violence and state-sponsored anti-Semitism in the Russian empire (which included large stretches of the historic Polish-Lithuanian Commonwealth, or Rzeczpospolita, with very sizable Jewish populations), and in particular the pogrom waves of 1881–82 and 1903–7, were the key driving forces pushing Jews to flee. This monocausal concept does not hold up to closer study, though the fact of particular pogroms may explain short-term upswings in migration—for example in the case of the Romanian pogroms of March 1907. It is better to look to multiple causes, not only official and popular anti-Semitism and its sporadic and scattered (and sometimes terrifying) violence, but more importantly the enormous shift in the traditional European economy and the impoverishment of much of its rapidly growing Jewish population. One must also keep in mind that the migrations to America were part of greater east–west and rural–urban movements of the European Jews.

The focus on Russian pogroms also means that the common narrative of American Jewish history focuses too tightly on German versus Russian periods and developments. Even beside the fact that significant numbers of Russian and other Eastern European Jews came before 1881–82, while German and other Western European Jews continued to arrive after 1882, patterns of Jewish settlement, faith, community, economics, and culture presented some remarkable continuities through the whole "long century" in America. Moreover, the most profound changes—for example in religious practices, beliefs, and other matters—affected all, regardless of exactly where they or their families came from. The American Jewish world that emerged by the early 1920s was an imagined community of extraordinary complexity.[2]

The rapid growth, diversity, and transformation of the American Jewish community—or rather, communities, both in the sense of particular locations and population groups—make the act of selecting texts and images a demanding task, given the limited space of this small volume. But some themes stand out and present a glimpse of critical concerns and the stages of Jews in America during the long nineteenth century. First, though it took place in the second half of the long century, we include the American Civil War, the event that shaped all of U.S. history: here texts and images from the Library's collections show that Jews of both the United States and the Confederacy chiefly followed their non-Jewish neighbors.

Then we proceed to the rich areas of Jewish life and culture that spanned the whole range of the long nineteenth century and that were truly interconnected. The first of this group comprises religious developments and change, including individuals, texts, and institutions. Examples are the first Hebrew Tanakh published in the U.S. (cat. 81) and its first translation (cat. 84); a small prayer book prepared for emigrants from Germany (cat. 85); and a series of articles that place a prominent German-born American rabbi in the Polish patriotic narrative (cat. 89). The next significant theme is the rising importance of social work and community, including the women's groups that emerged in these areas, as well as social and educational bodies. Among the examples are the 1825 Constitution of the Female Hebrew Benevolent Society of Philadelphia (cat. 92), and several publications by women's organizations from a century later. The chapter ends with a selection of items concerning Yiddish culture, including theater, literature, and the press, particular strengths of The New York Public Library's collections.

fig. 14
Portrait photograph of
Judah P. Benjamin,
ca. 1856

The Civil War 1861–65

cat. 69

Judah P. Benjamin (1811–1884)
*Relations of States: Speech of the Hon. J. P. Benjamin, of
Louisiana, Delivered in the Senate of the U.S., May 8, 1860: on
the Resolutions Submitted by the Hon. Jefferson Davis, of Miss.
on the 1st of March, 1860*
[Baltimore: Murphy & Co., 1860]

fig. 14

cat. 70

Judah P. Benjamin
Letter to Thomas Moore, October 1861
Page: 1

cat. 71

Judah P. Benjamin
*The African Slave Trade: The Secret Purpose of the Insurgents to
Revive It. No Treaty Stipulations Against the Slave Trade to Be
Entered into with the European Powers: Judah P. Benjamin's
Intercepted Instructions to L. Q. Lamar, Styled Commissioner,
Etc.*
Philadelphia: C. Sherman, Son & Co., printers, 1863

Judah P. Benjamin was the most important Jewish
official on either side of the Civil War. A senator from
Louisiana at the outbreak of the war, he became the
Confederacy's Secretary of War and then Secretary of
State, and was President Jefferson Davis's trusted and
capable friend and supporter. At the end of the war he
fled to England, where he became a successful specialist
in property law.

The New York Public Library holds several important
items representing Benjamin's activities. It preserves
pamphlets, such as his *Relations of States* (cat. 69),
supporting Davis. An October 1861 letter to Thomas
Moore, governor of Louisiana (cat. 70), states: "I am sure
you will be persuaded that nothing I can do shall be left
undone for the defense of Louisiana, whilst you would

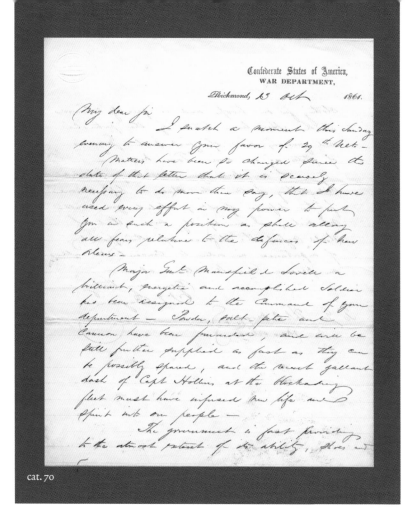

Confederate States of America,
WAR DEPARTMENT,
Richmond, 13 Oct 1861.

cat. 70

fig. 15
Official envelope decorated with a
portrait of Colonel Max Friedman,
of the same regiment as Rebekah
Hyneman's son, Elias Hyneman

Head-Quarters Cameron Dragoons.

Col. MAX FRIEDMAN.

fig. 15

not wish, I am equally sure, that I should neglect the defenses of other points of importance in order to concentrate *all* our resources on New Orleans alone" (that city fell to Union forces a few months later, one of the first great military disasters for the Confederacy). An 1863 booklet printed in Philadelphia (cat. 71) indicated, on the basis of Benjamin's confidential diplomatic instructions, that the Confederacy planned to revive the African slave trade, which had been banned decades before.

cat. 72

Rebekah Hyneman (1812–1875)
The Leper, and Other Poems
Philadelphia: A. Hart, 1853

Rebekah Hyneman, born to a Christian mother and a Jewish father, was raised a Jew. She published in Isaac Leeser's monthly journal, *The Occident*; this collection of poems is largely on Jewish Biblical themes. Her son, Elias Hyneman (1835–1865), enlisted in 1861 in the Union 5th Pennsylvania Cavalry regiment, largely organized in Philadelphia. A sergeant, he was captured in June 1864 during attacks on the railroads supplying Richmond and Petersburg, Virginia. He died at Andersonville prison camp, in Georgia, in February 1865 (of "debilitas," presumably general weakness and starvation, like many prisoners in that infamous camp), and is buried at the Andersonville National Historic Site cemetery. Post–Civil War pension files show that in 1875, the year of her own death, the mother applied for a pension on the basis of her son's service.

117

fig. 16

cat. 73

Phoebe Yates Pember (1823–1913)

A Southern Woman's Story

New York: G. W. Carleton & Co.; London: S. Low, Son &
Co., 1879

Phoebe Yates Levy Pember grew up in a prominent
Jewish family in Charleston, South Carolina. She later
lived in Savannah, Georgia. Widowed before the
outbreak of the Civil War, she became a nurse and
managing matron at Chimborazo Hospital in
Richmond, the largest Confederate military hospital;
this was a position of extraordinary responsibility for a
woman of this place and time. This memoir tells the
story of her experiences during the war. A contemporary
called her "brisk and brilliant": "Hers was a will of steel,
under a suave refinement, and her pretty, almost Creole
accent covered the power to ring in *defi* on occasion."[3]
One of her sisters, Eugenia Levy Phillips (1820–1902),
was a notorious Confederate sympathizer, expelled
from Washington, D.C., in 1861 and imprisoned in New
Orleans in 1862 for her actions. Their brother, Samuel
Yates Levy (1827–1888), an officer in the First Georgia
Infantry regiment, was captured in June 1864 during
the fighting for Atlanta; he survived imprisonment in
the north and remained a southern political partisan
after the war.

cat. 74

"General Grant's Order," *The Israelite*, vol. 9, no. 27
(January 9, 1863), p. 212

cat. 75

Ph. von Bort

General Grant and the Jews

New York: National News Co., [1868]

"General Order no. 11" of General Ulysses S. Grant (1822–
1885) remains notorious as the only official attempt in
American history to expel the entire Jewish population
of a particular territory. Dated December 17, 1862, in
Holly Springs, Mississippi, it reads:

The Jews, as a class violating every regulation of trade
established by the Treasury Department and also department
orders, are hereby expelled from the [U.S. Army's] department [of the
Tennessee] within twenty-four hours from the receipt of this order.

Post commanders will see that all of this class of people be
furnished passes and required to leave, and any one returning
after such notification will be arrested and held in confinement
until an opportunity occurs of sending them out as prisoners,
unless furnished with permit from headquarters.

No passes will be given these people to visit headquarters for
the purpose of making personal application for trade permits.

By order of Maj. Gen. U. S. Grant

Allegedly justified by Jewish criminal speculation in
and smuggling of contraband cotton, the order was probably connected to Grant's own father's attempt to profit,
with Jewish business partners, from his son's success.[4]
Whatever Grant's reasons, Jewish protests quickly reached
President Lincoln, who instructed that the order be re-
scinded. Grant's wife, Julia Dent Grant, referred to the
"obnoxious order" in her memoirs (published many years
later). General Order no. 11 became a political issue when
Grant ran for president in 1868. It is noteworthy that Grant
never again expressed such hostile views toward Jews, and
as president he took a number of steps to improve his relations with the Jewish community. These included the
appointment of a leader of the B'nai B'rith organization,
Benjamin Franklin Peixotto, as U.S. consul in Romania,
where there was considerable anti-Jewish pressure and

prejudice. The book by the pseudonymous P. von Bort
called on Jews to vote for Grant's Democratic Party opponent.

cat. 76

The American Jewish Seventy Elders
"Grant We Are Here Again": Thirty-Fifth Memorial Services for
General Grant: Sunday, August 15th, 1920
[New York: American Jewish Seventy Elders, 1920]

This brochure, with an image of Grant's Tomb, was
issued by a group called the American Jewish Seventy
Elders, whose name resonates in Jewish history, calling
to mind the Great Sanhedrin, the court of ancient Israel
that had seventy members. The program for the services
included a speech by Rabbi Edward B. M. Browne, a
politically active rabbi who had been among the pall
bearers at Grant's funeral in 1885.

cat. 77

Benjamin Szold (1829–1902)
Vaterland und Freiheit. Predigt bei der Erinnerungsfeier des
verstorbenen Präsidenten, Abraham Lincoln, am 1. Juni 1865,
dem zweiten Tag Shabuoth (Fatherland and freedom.
Sermon at the memorial celebration of the late
President, Abraham Lincoln, on June 1, 1865, the second
day of Shavuot)
[Baltimore]: Gedruckt bei W. Polmyer, 1865

Hebrew Confederate Soldiers Cemetery,
(North 5th St.,) Richmond, Va.

cat. 78

Born in Hungary, Benjamin Szold came to the United
States in 1859 to serve as rabbi at Congregation Oheb
Shalom in Baltimore. He and Marcus Jastrow
collaborated on German-language liturgies for their
synagogues. In this heartfelt sermon, preached during
the holiday of Shavuot, he calls on his congregants to
mourn Lincoln, even to "als einen Sohn Israels
betrachten"—regard him as a son of Israel. "Probably
the most poignant inspiration for preaching in
nineteenth-century America . . . was the assassination of
Abraham Lincoln. . . . Virtually every American rabbi
spoke on . . . 19 April, a national day of mourning, as
Lincoln's body was being taken to its burial place in
Illinois. These sermons reveal a sustained effort to
articulate the special qualities of Lincoln both as a
human being and as a political leader—sometimes

using explicitly messianic rhetoric—and later to apply
these qualities to the contemporary challenges of the body
politic."[5]

cat. 78

Hebrew Confederate Soldiers Cemetery
Richmond: Southern Bargain House, ca. 1907–15

This color postcard depicts this well-known cemetery. The
caption on the back of the card states: "This section of the
beautiful cemetery situated at the extreme end of North 5th
St. is under the care of the Hebrew Ladies Memorial
Association, of Richmond. Here are interred the remains of
many Jewish heroes who fell in the Civil War."

FIFTH AVENUE FROM 42ᴺᴰ STREET, LOOKING NORTH

cat. 79

Religious Developments

cat. 79

Robert A. Welcke (fl. 1878–1904), after the photograph
by John Bachmann (fl. 1849–1885)
Fifth Avenue from 42nd Street, Looking North
Chromolithograph, 1904

Temple Emanu-El, one of the largest and most historic
of American Reform Jewish congregations, held its first
services in 1845. As New York's Jewish population grew
and gained in strength and prosperity, this synagogue,
which was perhaps the quintessential German "our
crowd" congregation, moved uptown. This edifice, at
Fifth Avenue and East 43rd Street, opened in 1868.

John Bachmann's photograph of 1879 was the basis
of this print. The temple, with its twin Moorish spires, is
at the right foreground of the lithograph. This view was
probably taken from the top of the eight-story Hotel
Bristol, whose elaborate cornice is just visible in the left
foreground. From this towering vantage point, one
could have also looked down to the adjacent Croton
Reservoir to the south, now the site of The New York
Public Library's central building, today known as the
Stephen A. Schwarzman Building.

In 1927, Temple Emanu-El's congregation, which by
this time had merged with that of Temple Beth-El,
finished its present house of worship, the magnificent
Temple Emanu-El at Fifth Avenue and East 65th Street.
Its recently restored main sanctuary is the largest
synagogue space in the world—and many would say the
most beautiful, as well.

cat. 80

cat. 80

Mordecai M. Noah (1785–1851)
Travels in England, France, Spain, and the Barbary States in the Years 1813–14 and 15
New York: Kirk and Mercein, 1819
Page: Frontispiece portrait of Mordecai M. Noah, stipple engraving by Thomas Gimbrede after the painting by J. R. Smith

Noah, as mentioned earlier, was the most publicly prominent American Jew of his time; a writer, journalist, playwright, politician, and utopian (most notably proposing a Jewish refuge on Grand Island in the Niagara River, near Buffalo). He served as an American consul in Tunis, in North Africa, but then was removed from his position by Secretary of State James Monroe with the claim that the fact of his Jewish identity prevented his service. This caused a significant outcry, not least in American political circles.

cat. 81

תורה, נביאים וכתובים

Torah, Neviim u-Khetuvim: Biblia hebraica (Torah, prophets, and writings: Hebrew Bible) / *secundum ultimam editionem Jos. Athiae, a Johanne Leusden denuo recognitam, recensita variisque notis latinis illustrata ab Everardo van der Hooght, V.D.M.* (according to the latest edition of Jos. Athias, revised anew by Johannes Leusden, reviewed and illustrated with various Latin notes by Everardus van der Hooght, Minister of the Divine Word)
Philadelphia: Thomas Dobson and William Fry, 1814

This is the first Hebrew Bible (*Tanakh*) printed in the United States. It derives from the 1667 edition by Portuguese-born Amsterdam Jewish printer Joseph Athias (1634/35–1700) under the editorial supervision of Calvinist Hebraist Johannes Leusden (1624–1699), as edited later by another Protestant scholar, Everardus van der Hooght (1642?–1716). As Abraham Karp notes: "In some of the first copies off the press, an inserted page provides the history of its publication: 'In the year 1812, Mr. Horwitz had proposed the publication of an edition of the Hebrew Bible… The undertaking was strongly recommended by many clergymen…and a considerable number of subscriptions were obtained by him. Early in 1813, Mr. Horwitz transferred his right to the edition with his list of subscribers to Thomas Dobson, the present publisher.'"[6] This inserted page appears in the Library's copy.

fig. 17

fig. 18

cat. 82

Form of Service at the Dedication of the New Synagogue of the Kahal Kadosh Shearith Israel: in Crosby Street, New York

[New York]: S. H. Jackson, 5594 [1834]

Shearith Israel is the continuation of New York's first congregation. Its synagogue was moved progressively uptown through the decades, up to its current location at 70th Street and Central Park West. The photograph shows the synagogue on 19th Street between Ninth and Tenth avenues, its location from 1860 to 1897.

cat. 83

David Levi (ca. 1740–ca. 1800)

סדר הגדה של פסח :

מתורגם מלשון הקודש ללשון ענגלאטירא

Seder Hagadah shel Pesah: meturgam mi-leshon ha-kodesh li-leshon Englatera (Passover Haggadah: translated from Hebrew into English)

[New York: S. H. Jackson, 1836 or 1837]

This is the first Haggadah published in the United States. This English translation by David Levi was originally published in London in 1794.

cat. 85

cat. 84

Isaac Leeser (1806–1868)

תורת האלהים

Torat ha-Elohim (The law of God)

Philadelphia: C. Sherman, 5605 [1845]

Isaac Leeser, born in Germany, described himself as
Orthodox and a traditionalist, serving for many years at
the Mikveh Israel Synagogue in Philadelphia. This is
the first U.S.-published edition of the Pentateuch
translated from the Hebrew, which Leeser "edited, and
with former translations diligently compared and
revised." A prolific writer, he authored books for
children as well as translations and editions of prayer
books and the Hebrew scriptures, and also edited a
monthly journal, *The Occident*. Throughout his career,
Leeser stressed the importance of instruction in the
essentials of Judaism for Jews of all ages.

cat. 85

תפלה מכל השנה

מנחה קטנה

להולכי דרך ולעוברי ימים להנושעים למדינת אמעריקא
איינע מיניאטור אויזגאבע אויף פיינער פערל שריפט.

*Tefilah mi-Kol ha-Shanah Minhah Ketanah: le-holkhe derekh
ule-ovre yamim leha-nosim li-medinat Amerika: eyne
minyatur oyzgabe oyf fayner perl shrift* (The little sacrificial
offering, a prayer book for the whole year for travelers by
land and sea, for those making their way to the land of
America: a miniature edition set in fine five-point type)

[Fürth]: Verlag von S. B. Gusdorfer. Druck von J.
Sommer, 1860

Page: Title page

The title page of this miniature prayer book specifies its
intended audience as "travelers crossing the sea to the
nation of America." Originally issued in 1842, it was
reprinted several times, as America was becoming an
increasingly popular destination for European
emigrants. Between 1840 and 1860 many thousands of
Jews from Central Europe and other regions migrated to
the United States, with economic hardship, legal

fig. 19

fig. 19
Portrait photograph of Isaac
Mayer Wise, ca. 1880

limitations based on religious identity, and political
unrest as primary driving factors. During these years,
the estimated American Jewish population grew from
15,000 to 150,000. The words *minhah ketanah* (little
offering) in the title presumably allude both to the
volume's diminutive size and to its appropriateness as a
parting gift. The last phrase in the title (transliterated
as "eyne minyatur oyzgabe oyf fayner perl shrift," a
miniature edition set in five-point type) is in Yiddish,
rather than Hebrew.

cat. 86

Isaac Mayer Wise (1819–1900)

תפלות בני ישורון לראש השנה כפי מנהג אמעריקא

Tefilot Bene Yeshurun le-Rosh ha-shanah ke-fi minhag Amerika
(Prayers of [congregation] Bene Yeshurun for the New
Year, according to the American custom) / *The Divine
Service of American Israelites for the New Year*
Cincinnati: Bloch, 1866

Isaac Mayer Wise

תפלות בני ישורון ליום הכפורים כפי מנהג אמעריקא

*Tefilot Bene Yeshurun le-Yom ha-kipurim ke-fi minhag
Amerika* (Prayers of [congregation] Bene Yeshurun for
the Day of Atonement, according to the American
custom) / *The Divine Service of American Israelites for the
Day of Atonement*
Cincinnati: Bloch, 1866

As a young man Isaac Mayer Wise came to the United
States from Bohemia, a historic crown land of the
Austro-Hungarian empire. He began his rabbinic career
in Albany, New York, but is best known for his long
service in Cincinnati, where he played a key role in the
establishment of several institutions that later came to
define American Reform Judaism: the Union of
American Hebrew Congregations (now the Union for
Reform Judaism), Hebrew Union College (its seminary),
and the Central Conference of American Rabbis (its
main rabbinic organization). He also was an editor of
the weekly *The Israelite* and author of religious and
secular works. Most noteworthy here are the *machzorim*
(High Holidays liturgical books), which he prepared
"according to the American custom" (*ke-fi minhag
Amerika*). While Wise was to become associated with the
Reform movement specifically, his efforts were
originally attempts to unify American Jews and
Judaism.

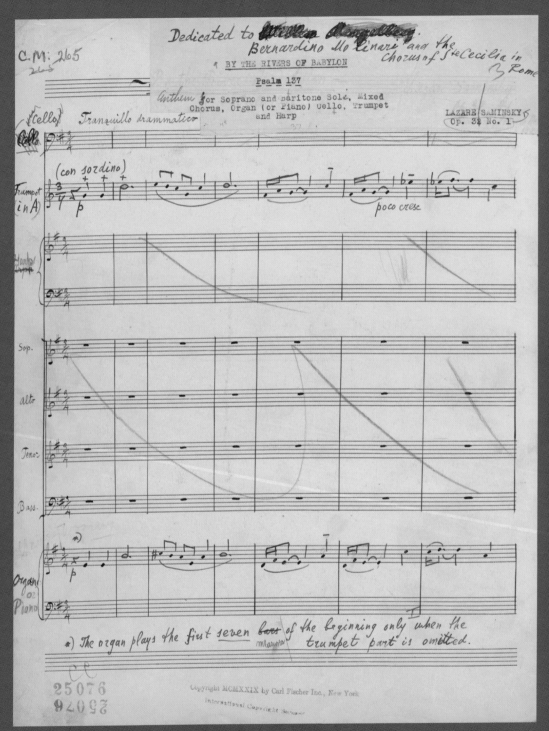

*) The organ plays the first seven bars of the beginning only when the trumpet part is omitted.

Copyright MCMXXIX by Carl Fischer Inc., New York

International Copyright Secured

cat. 87

Hymns Written for the Service of the Hebrew Congregation, Beth Elohim, Charleston S.C.
[Charleston]: Levin & Tavel, 1842

Congregation Beth Elohim was founded in the 1740s in Charleston, South Carolina, long one of the largest and most important Jewish communities in the British North American colonies and the young United States. In the first half of the nineteenth century this community saw conflicts over attempts to change or reform the service, among the first in America to experience this. Sixty of the seventy-four hymns in this collection were composed by Charleston native Penina Moise (1797–1880). She published secular poetry as well.

cat. 88

Lazare Saminsky (1882–1959)
"By the Rivers of Babylon: Psalm 137." Anthem for soprano and baritone soli, mixed chorus, organ (or piano), cello, trumpet, and harp: op. 33, no. 1
Chiefly holograph
New York, November 1926
Page: 1 of score

American synagogues drew on European professionals as well as on European models of architecture, liturgy, and service. New York's Temple Emanu-El, a classic example of a high "choral synagogue," is a case in point. Rather than hiring the best-known or most popular European cantors (such as Josef [Yossele] Rosenblatt, 1882–1933), who came to the United States seeking better salaries and improved working conditions, Emanu-El relied on professional music directors who served as composers, conductors, and even permanent scholars-in-residence. Lazare Saminsky, who served Emanu-El from 1924 on, was all of these. As a young musician in Russia, he was a student of the great composer Nikolai Rimsky-Korsakov (1844–1908) and an early member of the Society for Jewish Folk Music (*Obshchestvo Evreiskoi Narodnoi Muzyki*, in Russian), whose influence survives in the klezmer revival as well as in Israeli music. In the 1930s he played a leading role in the American-Palestine Institute of Musical Studies (MAILAMM, from its Hebrew initials). "By the Rivers of Babylon" is one of Saminsky's best-known pieces, and is still performed at Temple Emanu-El. A man of determined views, Saminsky wrote several books as well as secular and religious music, and did not hesitate to criticize sharply the works and views of his predecessors and contemporaries alike.

cat. 89

Marcus Jastrow (1829–1903)
"Bär Meisels, Oberrabbiner zu Warschau (Dov Berush Meisels, Chief Rabbi of Warsaw)," *The Hebrew Leader*, serialized in a series of 13 articles, vols. 15–16 (April–July 1870)

The career of Marcus Jastrow, who was born and educated in Germany, followed a remarkable path. Among leading American rabbis of the nineteenth century, his may be the most dramatic biography. As a young rabbi in the early 1860s, he served in Warsaw, Poland, which was then undergoing disturbances and eventually a failed armed uprising against its Russian rulers. In 1861, he was caught up in the unrest and spent months imprisoned in the city's dreaded Russian citadel, sometimes sharing a cell with the Orthodox official Chief Rabbi of Warsaw, Dov Berush Meisels. He described his experiences in later articles. He was subsequently expelled by the Russians, since he was a Prussian citizen. He briefly returned to Warsaw in 1862, but once the 1863 "January Insurrection" broke out in Poland, he was no longer allowed to return to the city.

One of his experiences became a very famous moment in the genre of Polish patriotic art. In 1861, five young demonstrators against Russian rule were killed, one of them a Jew. Jastrow, Meisels, and a third rabbi participated in the funeral procession for all the victims, which was led by the city's Catholic Archbishop-Metropolitan Antoni Melchior Fijalkowski. The event has been depicted in paintings. Perhaps the most

famous example is *The Funeral of the Five Victims in Warsaw of the Demonstration of 2 March 1861* (1866) by Aleksander Lesser (1814–1884), who was of Jewish ancestry. This event represented a high point in positive Polish-Jewish relations. Things deteriorated thenceforth, marked by the rise of an explicitly Polish anti-Semitic movement in the late nineteenth century.

Returning to Germany, Jastrow came to the United States in 1866, serving for many years at congregation Rodeph Shalom in Philadelphia. He became a recognized voice in German-language liturgy, for example editing revised prayer books. Later in life, Jastrow concentrated on his two-volume *Dictionary of the Targumim, the Talmud Babli and Yerushalmi, and the Midrashic Literature*, which is regarded as authoritative to this day. To summarize, this German-born rabbi, who spent most of his professional life in the United States and is perhaps best recalled for his dictionary prepared there, retains a uniquely positive image in Polish historiography and patriotic imagery.[7]

cat. 90

Baruch (Bernard) Poupko (1917–2010), editor
אידנו : ספר זכרון מוקדש לזכר רבנו הגאון ד"ר דוב רבל, ראש ישיבת רבנו יצחק אלחנן
Edenu: sefer zikaron mukdash le-zekher Rabenu ha-Gaon Dr. Dov Revel, rosh yeshivat Rabenu Yitshak Elhanan (Our distress: Memorial book for the illustrious Rabbi Dr. Bernard

cat. 91

Revel, President of the Rabbi Isaac Elchanan
Theological Seminary)
New York: Yeshiva College, 1942

Rabbi Bernard Dov Revel (1885–1940) was born in Russia
and as a young man was imprisoned by the Russian
authorities for revolutionary activities. Thus Marcus
Jastrow, considerably his senior, was not the only
prominent American rabbi to have that honor on his
resumé. Revel served as president of Yeshiva College
(now University) from 1915 to 1940, and was honored
with this memorial volume by his students.

cat. 91

Solomon Schechter (1847–1915)
Ex libris Solomon Schechter
Bookplate, ca. 1896–1915; Joseph B. Abrahams, designer

Solomon Schechter was born in Romania, received a university education in Germany, and then taught at Cambridge University and University College, London. He
gained international fame as a scholar in the 1890s when
he recovered hundreds of thousands of manuscripts,
mostly fragments, from the *geniza* (storeroom) of the Ben
Ezra synagogue, in Cairo, which for a thousand years had
been used as a repository of discarded manuscripts using
the Hebrew script. He was invited to be president of the
Jewish Theological Seminary in New York, which subsequently became the center of learning for the later American Conservative Jewish movement. He kept this position
until his death, and his influence on American Jewish
education and scholarship has proved to be lasting.

fig. 20

fig. 21

Community

cat. 92

The Constitution of the Female Hebrew Benevolent Society of Philadelphia

Philadelphia: J. H. Cunningham, 1825

Rebecca Gratz (1781–1869) was a founder of and is listed as the secretary of this society. She is probably the single most outstanding figure in nineteenth-century American Jewish education, charity, and philanthropy. From a prominent Pennsylvania business family, Gratz also founded the Hebrew Sunday School in Philadelphia and other organizations.

cat. 93

Maria Edgeworth (1767–1849)

Harrington, a Tale; and Ormond, a Tale

New York: Kirk and Mercein, 1817

Maria Edgeworth, a contemporary of Jane Austen, is remembered as the first important Irish novelist. In two early novels, *Castle Rackrent* (1800) and *The Absentee* (1812), she included unpleasant Jewish stereotypes. In particular, the latter novel has a character Mordicai, who is a vicious Jewish moneylender. After the book's publication, a reader, Rachel Mordecai Lazarus, a member of an important American Jewish family, wrote to Edgeworth, objecting to the portrayal. The chastened novelist replied: "Your polite, benevolent and touching letter has given me much pleasure, and much pain. As to the pain I hope you will see that it has excited me to make all the atonement and reparation in my power for the past."[8] Edgeworth then wrote another novel, *Harrington* (1817), featuring more positive (but still stereotyped) characters, and she and Lazarus continued a long and friendly correspondence.

cat. 94

Minna Kleeberg (1841–1878)

Gedichte (Poems)

Louisville: H. Knöfel; New York: Willmer u. Rogers News Co., 1877

fig. 20
Portrait of Rebecca Gratz, from "the miniature by Malbone, in possession of Mrs. Rebecca Gratz Nathan," reproduced in Gratz Van Rensselaer, "The Original of Rebecca in Ivanhoe," *The Century*, September 1882

fig. 21
Portrait of Maria Edgeworth, from "the original painting by Chappell in the possession of the publishers" Johnson, Wilson & Co., New York, stipple engraving, 1873

Minna Cohen Kleeberg was born in Germany, and came to the United States when her husband was given a rabbinic position in Louisville, Kentucky. She was already an established German-language poet, best known for "Ein Lied vom Salz" (A song of salt), a poem attacking the high state tax on salt in Prussia. In the U.S. she continued to write in German, publishing hymns in Isaac Mayer Wise's reformed hymnal, *Hymns, Psalms & Prayers* (1868), and poems in *Das New-Yorker Belletristische Journal* (The New York Belletristic Journal). *Gedichte*, her only published collection, appeared shortly before her death. The volume shows that she was influenced by American themes and scenes, with poems set at Niagara, and in Arkansas, Philadelphia, and Newport; and her poem "Der Jüdische Friedhof zu Newport," which she dedicated to Henry Wadsworth Longfellow, is a direct rejoinder to the great man's famous poem, "The Jewish Cemetery at Newport."

cat. 95

Emma Lazarus (1849–1887)
Songs of a Semite: The Dance to Death, and Other Poems
New York: Office of The American Hebrew, 1882

Emma Lazarus is among the most prominent American women poets of the nineteenth century. Her most famous poem, "The New Colossus," includes the memorable lines inscribed on a plaque on the pedestal of the Statue of Liberty: "Give me your tired, your poor, / Your huddled masses yearning to breathe free, / The wretched refuse of your teeming shore. / Send these, the homeless, tempest-tost to me, / I lift my lamp beside the golden door!" Deeply involved in the larger American literary world, she did not turn to Jewish themes until later in her career. She also became active in promoting early Zionist efforts and Jewish spiritual renewal, in part due to the shock of the 1881 Russian pogroms.

cat. 96

Mary Antin (1881–1949)
The Promised Land, with Illustrations from Photographs
Boston and New York: Houghton Mifflin, 1912

Mary Antin wrote two classics of American immigrant literature as a young woman: *From Plotzk to Boston* (1899) and *The Promised Land* (1912). In them she described her childhood in the Russian pale of settlement, her family's emigration to America, and her own personal success, facilitated when members of the Boston and New York literary elite discovered her abilities and ambitions. Later, she largely withdrew from public life, and published little, but her books have been republished and are still read as primary historical sources.

cat. 97

Official Correspondence Relating to Immigration of Russian Exiles
Washington, D.C.: Geso. R. Gray, 1891

In the last decades of the nineteenth century, Jewish immigration from Russia, Austria-Hungary, and elsewhere in Eastern Europe increased by great numbers. Hostility toward the immigrants, many of whom were poor as well as alien in practices and appearance, grew in American politics. This pamphlet represents an attempt by leading American Jewish organizations to prevent any attempt to exclude many immigrants on the grounds of poverty, demonstrating the concern that established Jewish communities had for the new—and typically poorer—arrivals. It is headed, "Plans of action of: Independent Order B'nai B'rith, Jewish Alliance of America, Baron de Hirsch [Fund] Trustees, [and the] Union of American Hebrew Congregations." The pamphlet is a response to an act of Congress dated March 3, 1891, which threatened that "when expatriated Russian refugees seek asylum in this country if there is any risk of their being likely to become a public charge they must be excluded from admission in to the United States." The four organizations listed above proposed to prove, with their response, "that the expatriated Russians … should not be classed as paupers," and therefore should not be excluded from the country (pp. 1–2).

cat. 98

Amelia Greenwald (1881–1966)
Manual for Field Workers
New York: Committee on Farm Work, the Council of Jewish Women, ca. 1923

Amelia Greenwald, an internationally active public health nurse, was national organizer and director of the Committee on Work for Women on Farms. Born in Gainesville, Alabama, she served in World War I and worked in Poland as well as in many positions of responsibility in the United States. In the foreword to this booklet, she writes: "The purpose of the Council of Jewish Women's Farm Work is to know the Jewish women living on the farms and in the rural districts, and to extend to them a hand of fellowship; to bring to them the inspiring assurance of the Council's appreciation of Farm Women's part in the development of this great land which offers to all freedom, peace and happiness; and their contribution to the achievements of Jewish Womanhood." The work of the committee was part of broader efforts to move more immigrant Jews out of American cities and into farming and rural environments. The National Council of Jewish Women, founded in 1893 on the occasion of the Chicago World's Fair, is one of the oldest social aid organizations in the Jewish context.

EDUCATIONAL ALLIANCE, EAST BROADWAY, NEW YORK.
(From a photograph.) #458

fig. 22

cat. 99

Handbook for Jewish Women's Organizations
New York: Women's League of the United Synagogue,
1924

The United Synagogue of America was formed as the
umbrella organization for the Conservative movement
in American Judaism. This booklet represents rules and
procedures for local groups of the Women's League of
the United Synagogue, the founding president of which
was Mathilde Roth Schechter (1857–1924), Solomon
Schechter's wife (see cat. 91). The introduction is by

Deborah M. Melamed (1892–1954), a rabbi's wife known
as the author of *The Three Pillars: Thought, Worship and
Practice for the Jewish Woman* (1927), a highly regarded
work that went through a number of printings.

cat. 100

Elma Ehrlich Levinger (1887–1958)
*The Tower of David: A Book of Stories for the Program of
Women's Organizations*
New York: Bloch Publishing Company, 1924

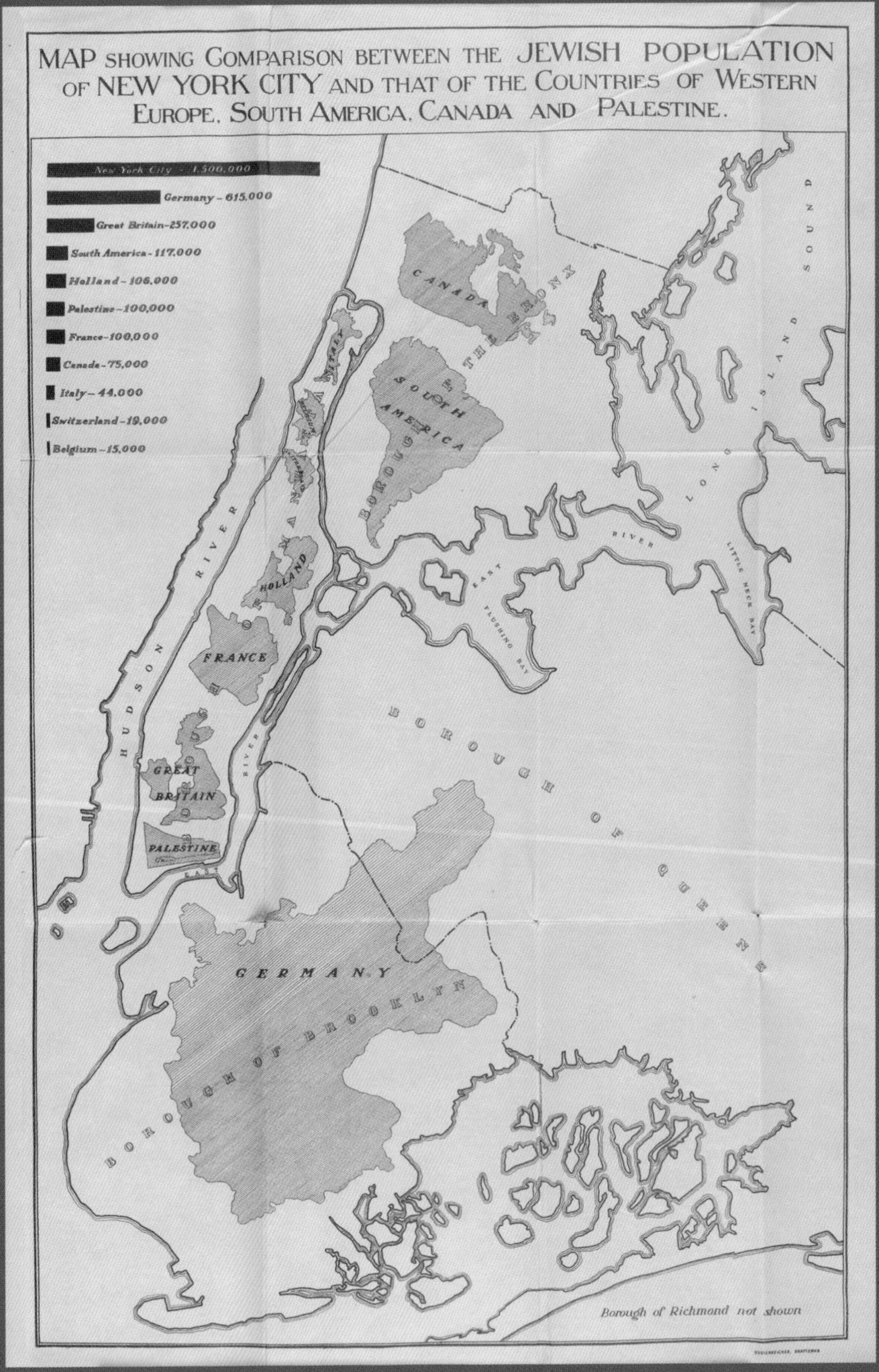

MAP SHOWING COMPARISON BETWEEN THE JEWISH POPULATION OF NEW YORK CITY AND THAT OF THE COUNTRIES OF WESTERN EUROPE, SOUTH AMERICA, CANADA AND PALESTINE.
New York City - 1,500,000
Germany - 615,000
Great Britain-257,000
South America - 117,000
Holland - 106,000
Palestine - 100,000
France - 100,000
Canada - 75,000
Italy - 44,000
Switzerland - 19,000
Belgium - 15,000
CANADA
THE BRONX
SOUTH AMERICA
LONG ISLAND SOUND
HUDSON RIVER
HOLLAND
FRANCE
GREAT BRITAIN
PALESTINE
EAST RIVER
FLUSHING BAY
LITTLE NECK BAY
BOROUGH OF QUEENS
GERMANY
BOROUGH OF BROOKLYN
Borough of Richmond not shown

cat. 101

Elma Ehrlich Levinger, born in Chicago, was a teacher who wrote promoting Jewish education. This book, sponsored by the National Council of Jewish Women, presents a number of didactic Jewish-themed stories to be used and adapted for various women's programs and organizations.

cat. 101

פנקס הקהלה דנויארק רבתי

The Jewish Communal Register of New York City, 1917–1918 / Pinkas ha-Kehilah de-Nuyork rabati, 678
New York: Kehillah (Jewish Community) of New York City, 1918

Directories often include a wealth of primary information documenting the growth and changes in communities, and their adaptations to the American environment. For American Jews in New York (and elsewhere), most noteworthy was the decentralized nature of the community, in which individuals and groups could define themselves and make their own arrangements, independent of both governments and established religious bodies. The preface to this massive work states the need: "New York is the heart of American Jewry.... And yet the one essential to make permanent the gains thus far made, and to ensure progress in the future, is sorely lacking—the community is not sufficiently conscious of itself. The community does not really know itself.... What, then, is the first duty of those who would bring order out of chaos in the communal life of the Jews in New York City?" (p. iii). One answer was this exhaustive directory, with 1,597 pages of small print. The Kehillah—this is the traditional term for a Jewish communal organization—only lasted from 1908 to 1922. The register was based on a "comprehensive demographic, economic, and institutional survey of New York Jewry. ... The communal portrait that emerged confirmed well-known facts about the prevailing situation: on the one hand, institutional complexity and confusion, parochialism, and extreme decentralization; on the other hand, the existence of vast resources and abundance of common weal."[9]

fig. 23

Yiddish Popular Culture: Literature, Theater, and the Press

One of the most striking aspects of the enormous growth and development of the American Jewish community was the extent to which it coincided with an explosion of popular, vernacular Yiddish culture. Yiddish newspapers provided Eastern European Jewish immigrants with news, editorials, advice, advertisements, community announcements, and literature. The Dorot Jewish Division has played a pioneering role in microfilming its comprehensive holdings of periodicals: microfilmed American Yiddish newspapers peak at fifty-seven titles in the 1920s (compared to the division's seventy-one English, four Hebrew, and four Ladino periodicals from the same period). New York's daily Yiddish newspapers *Forverts* (Forward; popularly known as the *Jewish Daily Forward*), *Tog* (The Day), and *Morgen-zshurnal* (Morning Journal) form the best-known triumvirate, while dozens of other newspapers were published in Boston, Chicago, Cleveland, Detroit, Los Angeles, Milwaukee, Newark, Philadelphia, Pittsburgh, Portland (Oregon), San Francisco, and New York itself. Each paper had its own political and religious orientation, from anarchist to communist to religiously observant, sometimes all at once. The humor magazine *Der groyser kundes* (The big stick, 1909–27) poked fun at it all with elaborate parodies and comics.

Other Yiddish publications, representing the richness of communal life, proliferated during the early twentieth century. Professional, trade, and labor journals addressed diverse subjects, including baking (*Idishe bekers shtime*, 1917–60; Yiddish bakers' voice); Yiddish theater (*Idishe bihne*, 1910; Yiddish stage); farming (*Idisher farmer*, 1911–59; Jewish farmer); the garment industry (*Kloth, het, kep, un millineri voyrkers zshurnal*, 1916–17; Cloth, hat, cap, and millinery workers'

fig. 23

Poster for **דיא אלרייטניקעס**
/ *Di alraytnikes* (The all-
rightniks), Kessler's
Thalia Theatre, 46–48
Bowery, New York,
March 4–6, 1910

journal); women's issues (*Idisher froyen zshurnal*, 1922–23; Jewish women's journal); and education (*Kinder zshurnal*, 1920–74; Children's journal; and *Kinderland*, 1921–23; Children's land). *Landsmanshaftn* (hometown associations) published souvenir pamphlets, constitutions, and journals, such as the *Byalistoker Shtime* (Bialystok voice), tangibly demonstrating the bond between immigrants from the same city while raising money for charity in Europe. Yiddish educational institutions published pedagogical materials, juvenile literature, and periodicals as part of a national network of supplementary schools.

Yiddish poetry and fiction flourished in the U.S. during the early twentieth century in newspapers, journals, and books. Daily newspapers enticed readers with suspenseful serialized novels, short stories, and poetry. The work of Morris Rosenfeld, Morris Winchevsky, David Edelstadt, and Joseph Bovshover, the so-called "sweatshop poets," moved audiences with its impassioned and sympathetic descriptions of workers' lives. Literary periodicals included *Di Tsukunft* (The future), the oldest and still-running Yiddish literary journal; *Yugend* (Youth), founded by an innovative group of young Yiddish poets; and *In zikh* (In oneself), a journal of the introspective Yiddish poetry movement.

Beginning with cheap popular romance novels, American Yiddish publishing featured the works of the three classic Yiddish writers, Mendele Moykher Sforim,

Y. L. Peretz, and Sholem Aleichem, and, later, the poetry and fiction of American Yiddish writers like Sholem Asch, I. J. Singer, and Joseph Opatoshu, as well as the landmarks of world literature translated into Yiddish. Women's contributions to Yiddish literature came later; novelist Miriam Karpilove (nos. 102–4) played a pioneering role with her serialized novels in the Yiddish press, while Anna Margolin and introspectivist Celia Drapkin led the poets in the 1920s. Ezra Korman's *Yidishe dikhterins* (Jewish poetesses) (cat. 105), a groundbreaking anthology of female Yiddish poets, was published in 1928.

American Yiddish theater arose with mass immigration from Eastern Europe, developing into a major industry and cultural phenomenon, with New York's Second Avenue as the city's Yiddish Broadway, and productions in cities across the country, including Baltimore, Chicago, Cleveland, Detroit, Los Angeles, and Newark. Boris Thomashefsky is credited with founding the American Yiddish theater, legendary both for his flamboyant personality and the elaborate productions that both he and his wife (later ex-wife and rival), Bessie Thomashefsky, often starred in. The ban on Yiddish theater in Russia drew actors Jacob P. Adler, Bertha Kalish, David Kessler, Sigmund Mogulesco, Sophia Karp, and Keni Liptzin to America. Playwrights Joseph Lateiner, "Professor" Moshe Horowitz, and Shomer churned out light fare for the masses, while Jacob Gordin strove to create serious classic drama. In

the 1920s, Molly Picon gained fame with her spry
gymnastics, boyish disguises and pixie-like charm.
Composers Joseph Rumshinsky, Sholom Secunda, and
Alexander Olshanetsky wrote hundreds of songs and
scores, published by Metro Music, Hebrew Publishing
Company, and the Kammen Brothers, and sold as sheet
music at performances. Sadly, the works of playwright,
lyricist, and composer Abraham Goldfaden, known as
the father of Yiddish theater, were performed and
printed in the U.S. without copyright protection, and he
died penniless in New York in 1908.

cat. 102

Miriam Karpilove (1888–1956)
טאַגע-בוך פֿון אַ עלענדע מיידעל, אָדער, דער קאַמפּף
געגען פֿרײַע ליעבע
*Tage-bukh fun a elende meydel, oder, Der kampf gegen fraye
liebe* (Diary of a lonely girl, or, the struggle against
free love)
New York: S. Kantrowitz, ca. 1910s

cat. 103

Miriam Karpilove
יהודית : אַ געשיכטע פֿון ליעבע און לײַדען
Yehudit: a geshikhte fun liebe un layden (Yehudis: a story of
love and suffering)
New York: Mayzel et k|o., 1911

cat. 104

Miriam Karpilove
אין דיא שטורם טעג
In di shturm teg (In the stormy days)
New York, 1909
Page: Title page, with portrait photograph of Miriam
Karpilove

Miriam Karpilove was a prolific novelist who focused
on the lives and emotional struggles of Jewish
immigrant women and girls in America. She was one
of the few women to earn a living as a Yiddish writer,
chiefly publishing in New York daily newspapers and
periodicals. She mostly wrote serials; only a few of
her novels ever appeared in book form, and none of
her longer works have been translated into English.

cat. 105

Ezra Korman (1888–1959), editor
ייִדישע דיכטערינס : אַנטאָלאָגיע
Yidishe dikhterins: antologye (Jewish poetesses: an
anthology)
Chicago: L. M. Shtayn, 1928

This famous collection disproves the notion that
women have contributed little to Yiddish literature.
In fact, for centuries, writing in Yiddish was by and
for women more than it was for men, who were
expected to know Hebrew. Ezra Korman was

572669

אין דיא שטורם טעג

דראמא אין 4 אקטען

פון

מרים קארפילאוו

נאכדרוק אדער אויפפיהרונג שטרענג פערבאטען.

פרייז 15 סענט.

associated with the artistically and politically radical post–World War I *Kultur-Lige* (culture league), which was affiliated with socialist and communist elements in the Soviet Union and Poland. By the time this book was published, he had settled in Detroit. The anthology opens with works written in "the Old Yiddish (1600–1800)," then proceeds with the "New Yiddish (1888–1927) literature," and concludes with biographical and bibliographical notes. Photostats of the early works and portraits of the poets are included. The New York Public Library's copy, according to a plate attached to the inside of the volume's cover, was a gift from the publisher on May 10, 1928.

cat. 106

די צוקונפֿט

Di Tsukunft (The future)
New York: Aroysgegebn fun dem Alvelt. Yiddishn
kultur-kongres, 1892–

Di Tsukunft began life in New York in 1892 as a journal of
the Socialist Labor party, and soon became one of the
most important Yiddish literary and intellectual
periodicals of any place or persuasion. From 1912 to 1940
it was issued by the publishers of the daily *Forverts*
(Forward), and since then by the Central Yiddish
Cultural Organization (better known as CYCO) and the
Congress for Jewish Culture. *Di Tsukunft* still appears on
a semiannual basis.

cat. 107

דער גרױסער קונדס

Der groyser kundes (The big stick)
New York: Jewish Pub. and Advertising Co., 1909–27
Page: Front page of the issue of April 26, 1912 (vol. 17, no. 17)

The Yiddish humor magazine *Der groyser kundes* specialized
in parodying self-consciously serious newspapers and
periodicals such as *Di Tsukunft* (cat. 106). The issue of
April 26, 1912, seen here, took the recent tragedy of the
Titanic sinking as fodder for wide-ranging satire.

cat. 108

Sholom Secunda (1894–1974), music; **Sholom Ben
Avrohom** (a pseudonym for Sholom Secunda?), words

חזנים אױף פּראָבע

Hazonim oyf probe / Chazonim oif probe (Cantors at the
audition). Song for voice and piano
New York: Metro Music Co., ca. 1935

cat. 109

Sholom Secunda, music; **Chaim Tauber** (1901–1972),
lyrics; **Oscar Ostroff** (1904–1979), libretto

אַ שפּיל אין ליבע : אָפּערעטט אין צװײי
אַקטען אין 4 בילדער

A shpil in libe: operett in tsvey akten in 4 bilder (A game of
love: opera in two acts and four scenes)
New York(?), ca. 1935

Sholom Secunda, born in Russian-ruled Ukraine, came
to the United States as a child. Performing as a boy
prodigy cantor until his voice changed, he studied
music and worked as a composer for the Yiddish theater
in New York. He is best known for comic and light pieces
in Yiddish, some of which were translated and became
hits in English. Examples of the latter include "Bay mir
bistu sheyn," transliterated into a kind of quasi-German
as "Bei mir bist du schoen" ("To me you are beautiful"),
first recorded in an English version by the Andrews
Sisters in 1937; and "Dos kelbl" ("The calf"), with lyrics
by Aaron Zeitlin (1898–1973), known in English as

cat. 107

"Dona Dona" and an antiwar hit for Joan Baez (and others) in the 1960s. The two selections here are a comic piece, "Cantors at the Audition," and an operetta, *A Game of Love*. In *Funny, It Doesn't Sound Jewish*, Jack Gottlieb suggests that "Sholom Ben Avrohom," the lyricist of the comic song, is perhaps a pseudonym for Sholom Secunda himself.[10]

fig. 24

fig. 25

cat. 110

The Thomashefsky Collection

Bores (or Boris) Thomashefsky (1866–1939)

Bores Thomashefsky, born near Kiev, started in the New York Yiddish theater as a teenager and became the biggest individual star of that stage. Besides the light material for which the Yiddish theater was chiefly known, he also performed Shakespeare in Yiddish translation. The New York Public Library's Thomashefsky collection includes his Yiddish scripts of *Hamlet, prints fun Denmark* (Hamlet, Prince of Denmark), *Keneg Rikhard der III* (King Richard III), *Kenig Lier* (King Lear), *Koriolanus: troyershpil* (The Tragedy of Coriolanus), *Otello* (Othello), *Romeo un Yulye* (Romeo and Juliet), and *Shaylok* (Shylock, presumably *The Merchant of Venice*).

fig. 24
Bores Thomashefsky photographed by White Studio, New York, in his operetta *Dos Tsubrokhene fiedele* (The broken violin), music by Joseph Rumshinsky, first produced October 11, 1916, at the National Theater on Second Avenue

fig. 25
Theater placard advertising a performance of Bores Thomashefsky's *Der Griner Boher* (The green boy) at the People's Theatre, 201 Bowery, Thursday evening, February 16, 1905. The play, with Thomashefsky's wife in the title role, promised: "An amusing evening for all theater visitors and friends. A New York holiday! A happy holiday! An honest holiday! Madame Bessie Thomashefsky's benefit. . . . A present: everyone who buys a ticket for this performance will receive as a present an impressive souvenir photograph of Madame Bessie Thomashefsky in one of her poses."

cat. 112

cat. 111

Molly Picon (1898–1992), words; **Joseph Rumshinsky** (1881–1956), music

אַ ביסעל ליעבע און אַ ביסעלע גליק

"A bisel liebe un a bisele glik" (A little love and a little happiness)

New York: Sani Shapiro, ca. 1924

This song was written for Rumshinsky's musical *Tzipke*. Molly Picon was one of the biggest stars of the Yiddish stage and film. Later in life, she appeared in a number of television shows and English-language movies, including *Fiddler on the Roof* (1971). Born near Vilnius, Joseph Rumshinsky began working as a professional composer and conductor in Russia at a young age. Coming to America in 1904, he became one of the biggest names in the Yiddish musical theater, collaborating frequently with Picon, Thomashefsky, and other stars.

fig. 26
Portrait photograph
of Jennie Goldstein
by Rappoport, New
York, ca. mid–late
1920s

cat. 112

Molly Picon, words; **Joseph Rumshinsky**, music

דו ביזט מײַן גליק

"Du bist mein glick" / "Du bizt mayn glik" (You are my
happiness)
New York: [Trio Press], ca. 1920s
Page: Sheet music cover

This music was written for Rumshinsky and Jacob Kalich's
Di komediantke (The little clown). Kalich was Picon's
husband.

cat. 113

Jennie Goldstein (1896–1960), words; **Harry Lubin**
(1906–1977), music

ווי אַ חלום איז אַלעס אַוועק

"Vi a holem iz ales avek" / "Just Like a Dream"
New York: Trio Press, 1928

The song "Vi a holem iz ales avek" / "Just Like a Dream"
was written for *A meydel mit a fargangenheyt* (A girl with a
past). Jennie Goldstein, a star in the Yiddish theater, was
best known for tragic roles.

fig. 26

Notes

1. British historian Eric Hobsbawm is particularly associated with the concept of the "long nineteenth century" in European history, in a three-volume series of surveys of European history covering precisely 1789–1914: *The Age of Revolution: Europe, 1789–1848* (London: Weidenfeld & Nicholson, 1962), *The Age of Capital, 1848–1875* (London: Weidenfeld & Nicholson, 1975), and *The Age of Empire, 1875–1914* (London: Weidenfeld & Nicholson, 1987).

2. Benedict Anderson, in his concise book *Imagined Communities: Reflections on the Origin and Spread of Nationalism*, 2nd rev. ed. (New York: Verso, 1991), articulated this powerful concept, which has revolutionized studies of nationality, colonialism, and the responses of the colonized and subaltern populations to their situations.

3. T. C. De Leon, *Belles, Beaux and Brains of the 60's* (New York: G. W. Dillingham Company, 1909), 385.

4. See Jonathan D. Sarna, *When General Grant Expelled the Jews* (New York: Random House, 2012).

5. Marc Saperstein, *Jewish Preaching in Times of War, 1800–2001* (Oxford, England and Portland, Or.: Littman Library of Jewish Civilization, 2008), 9. A sizable number of these and other sermons are collected in Emanuel Hertz, ed., *Abraham Lincoln: The Tribute of the Synagogue* (New York: Bloch, 1927).

6. Abraham Karp, "The Hebrew Book in the New World: From Bibliography to History," Association of Jewish Libraries, Rosaline and Myer Feinstein Lecture Series, 2000: p. [5]. www.jewishlibraries.org. Karp adds that this "was not in fact the first proposal" to publish the Hebrew scriptures in the U.S.

7. For a book-length biography in Polish, see Michal Galas, *Rabin Markus Jastrow i jego wizja reformy judaizmu: studium z dziejów judaizmu w XIX wieku* (Kraków: Austeria, 2007).

8. Edgar E. MacDonald, ed., *The Education of the Heart: The Correspondence of Rachel Mordecai Lazarus and Maria Edgeworth* (Chapel Hill: University of North Carolina Press, 1977), 8.

9. Arthur A. Goren, *New York Jews and the Quest for Community: The Kehillah Experiment, 1908–1922* (New York: Columbia University Press, 1970), 236–37.

10. Jack Gottlieb, *Funny, It Doesn't Sound Jewish: How Yiddish Songs and Synagogue Melodies Influenced Tin Pan Alley, Broadway, and Hollywood* (Albany: State University of New York in association with the Library of Congress, 2004), 175, note 2.

DUX

The Dorot Jewish Division
of The New York Public Library

The history and development of the Jewish collections at The New York Public Library in many ways reflect the rise and transformation of the New York Jewish community. The Jewish collections arose as distinctive holdings at the end of the nineteenth century, early in the history of the newly established Library. Many of the Library's existing Judaica holdings, including those from the Astor and Lenox private libraries and from the Aguilar Library, a private library foundation that chiefly served Manhattan's Jewish community, were consolidated into a new department for Semitic and Oriental collections at The New York Public Library. This was subsequently split into the Jewish (or Semitic, or Hebrew) and the Oriental departments.

The Jewish Department was greatly supported and augmented by financial gifts to an important acquisitions fund established by Jacob H. Schiff (1847–1920), a German-born banker and businessman who immigrated to the United States as a young man and became a prominent figure in New York's financial world. His philanthropic undertakings—supporting practically every major Jewish educational institution in New York—are especially noteworthy. Schiff's fund supported the acquisition of "Semitic literature" for the Library; over a century later, the fund's purchasing power has diminished substantially, but it still generates income used to purchase books for the Dorot Jewish Division.

Abraham S. Freidus (1867–1923), an immigrant from Russia who began work as a cataloger of Hebrew books,

became the first official chief of the Jewish Division, serving until his death in 1923. He seems to have been a remarkable and brilliant character, although this account also attests to his reputation as a comic one:

He compiled all sorts of special indexes and clipping files and devised an elaborate and influential scheme for his collection. He was an impassive storehouse of information on all things Jewish, a bookworm and bookbuyer rather than an administrator, utterly devoted to his work. . . . He apparently had his troubles with [Library director John] Billings, to whom he finally appealed to end the "tragedy" of the "extreme torture of being continually branded a delinquent" while he was giving his life to the library. The difficulty probably lay in Freidus' incorrigible inability to deliver work on time and his indifference to order and system.[1]

A 1944 remembrance of Freidus, while acknowledging his role as a "great custodian," presents him somewhat unkindly as a broadly comic figure.[2] A more authoritative figure, Harry Lydenberg, who was head of reference at the Library in Freidus's last years and who eventually became its director, recalled: "He was no administrator, and he had not the slightest idea of how to plan work for others and how to get it accomplished. . . . He had not the slightest sense of order, not the slightest conception of the help that order and system give towards attainment of results. But he was a bookman. He did get a real pleasure from putting books to use and

fig. 28

from digging up from their sometimes dusty depths things to help the wanderer along the road, who lacked that knowledge and ability Freidus possessed so thoroughly."[3] Some of the disorder of the day can be seen in the comment that the division under Freidus more resembled a *kloizl*—an East European Yiddish term for a small prayer and study room,[4] typically envisioned as crowded, chaotic, and loud.

Despite all this, Freidus also was able to create a classification system for the Jewish Division that was both modern and scientifically sound, one that has been used in other Jewish library collections as well.[5] The significance of this should not be underestimated. A later writer noted that this "newfangled classification scheme was as much a symbolic gesture as a practical one. For when it came to matters of cultural taxonomy, the formation of the Jewish Division betokened growing awareness that not only did the Jews have a culture all their own, but that this culture was very much a part of Western civilization."[6] It seems appropriate that one of the early frequent readers was Eliezer Ben-Yehuda, the creator of the modern Hebrew language, who spent some years in the division working on his monumental *Dictionary of the Ancient and Modern Hebrew Language* (1908–59). The division also served as a base for the great *Jewish Encyclopedia* (1901–6), the first work of its kind to be prepared and published in English.

Up to the moment of his sudden death of a heart attack on the steps of the Library, Freidus played a critical role in the collection's beginnings; he was paid tribute as "a remarkable and unique personality who left a lasting impression upon the intellectual life of American Jewry."[7]

His eventual success was, at first glance, an unlikely outcome. Born in Riga, now in Latvia, Freidus had maskilic ambitions—that is, to be a follower of the Haskalah, the Jewish secularizing enlightenment that began in eighteenth-century Germany. As a young man, he went to Ottoman-ruled Palestine and worked, evidently not very successfully, as an "idealist farm worker." He then moved on to Paris, again without finding any success. He came to America in 1889; "after several years of drifting" he took the librarian course at the Pratt Institute in Brooklyn (then still an

fig. 29
Frontispiece portrait of Joshua
Bloch, from *The Joshua Bloch
Memorial Volume: Studies in Booklore
and History*, ed. Abraham Berger,
Lawrence Marwick, and Isidore S.
Meyer (New York: The New York
Public Library, 1960)

independent city), finishing in 1894. Shortly afterward
he came to The New York Public Library, which became
his home for the rest of his life.

Almost a century after his death, Freidus's legacy
lives on in the fact that the present-day Dorot Jewish
Division uses freidus@nypl.org as its e-mail address for
public questions, reflecting a lingering fondness for the
first chief's foibles.

Freidus's successor, Joshua Bloch (1890–1957), was
more of a scholar, and served for over thirty years in the
position (1923–56). Under Bloch, "the Jewish Division
began to shed some of its informality, becoming more
professional ... more like the reading room of the
British Museum.... For thirty-three years, Dr. Bloch
presided over the 'Jewish room,' transforming it from a
kloizl into a 'mecca,' one of his favorite words."[8] "When
he took over ... he found a small, difficult-to-use
collection. He left a collection consisting of 110,000
volumes, with a richly cross-indexed catalogue of half a
million entries."[9]

Born in Russian-ruled Lithuania, Bloch came to the
United States in 1907. He studied variously at Hebrew
Union College (where he became a rabbi), Dropsie
College, Jewish Theological Seminary, Union
Theological Seminary, and Columbia University, finally
receiving his doctorate from New York University. His
own research interests were in the areas of Hebrew book
and print studies, apocalyptic literature, Syriac
literature, and the history of the Musar movement (an

fig. 29

ethical and religious movement among nineteenth-
century Russian Jews). His dissertation was "a critical
examination of the text of the Syriac version of the *Song
of Songs*,"[10] and his avowedly incomplete professional
bibliography includes 415 entries. Eventually he added
the field of American Jewish studies to his interests; his
"American Jewish Literature: A Tercentenary Review"
remains a very useful summary of the topic.[11] In the

Memorial Volume published in Bloch's honor, the author Anita Libman Lebeson acknowledged, "In many conferences he helped clarify and interpret the role of the Jew in the building of America."[12]

Among his most noteworthy achievements was the exhibition *The Background of Three Hundred Years of Jewish Life in America*. Its catalogue was published in 1954 as *The People and the Book*.[13] The exhibition sought to reveal "the character and cultural value of the great spiritual treasures Jews carried with them from place to place in every land of their sojourn and in every age. The ideas and ideals these treasures embody found deep roots in American life."[14]

Bloch became an important figure in the rise of American Jewish studies not only through his writings and his management of the Library's Jewish Division. He was very active professionally in numerous organizations, including the Jewish Book Council, the Jewish Publication Society, the American Jewish Historical Society, and two major rabbinic bodies: the New York Board of Rabbis and the Central Conference of American Rabbis.[15] He died shortly after his retirement, while leading a Rosh-Hashanah service in his capacity as Rabbinic Chaplain at Creedmoor State Hospital in Queens.

The development of the Slavonic and Baltic collections (chiefly covering works in Russian and other Slavic languages) was, at the beginning, linked to that of the Jewish collections. The history of those collections therefore deserves a brief mention. Before the turn of the twentieth century, "[t]wo noted divisions of the Reference Department, the Jewish and Slavonic, represent in part Billings' recognition of the status of New York as the leading Jewish community in the United States."[16] This early connection was based on the fact that a very large proportion of Jewish immigration to New York came from the Russian empire; and conversely, almost all Russian intellectuals in the city were Jews, or at least of Jewish ancestry.

The Slavonic Department was founded in 1898–99, its first chief being Herman Rosenthal (1843–1917), a Russian-Jewish poet, author (in Hebrew as well as Russian and German), printer, and translator from Kurland (now part of Latvia) who came to the United States in 1881. In 1881–82 he helped found Jewish agricultural colonies for immigrants in Louisiana, South Dakota, and Woodbine, New Jersey, under the direction of Baron Maurice de Hirsch, the key figure in efforts at Jewish resettlement in the wake of the pogroms of 1881 in Russia. Rosenthal subsequently held a number of professional positions in and around New York City. He also was active in the early Zionist movement, and served on the board of the *Jewish Encyclopedia*. Thoroughly versed in Slavic languages as well as German and Hebrew, he was hailed as "a man of broad general culture."[17] Serving subsequently as head of the Slavonic Department from 1918 to 1955, Avrahm Yarmolinsky (1890–1975) was another Russian-born

Jewish intellectual; he published extensively in Russian history, literature, and bibliography, and taught at New York–area universities.[18] The Slavonic Department became one of the leading collections of (primarily) Russian-language library holdings in the United States, though its links to the Library's Jewish collections weakened.

Under subsequent curators, the collections of the Jewish Division continued to grow by the purchase and gift of books and other materials, and through the contributions of donor funds as well as the regular general support of the Library. In 1983, for example, a gift from the estate of New York City realtor Jacob Perlow established an endowment fund that partially supports acquisitions, conservation, and public services. In 1986, the Dorot Foundation endowed the position of the chief of the division (this foundation still generously supports the division), and the following year the S. H. and Helen R. Scheuer Family Foundation made a substantial gift for renovation and new technology. The Nash Family Foundation has also been very supportive in recent years.

Writing in his foreword to *A Sign and a Witness*, a 1988 collection of essays based on an important exhibition at the Library, its president, Vartan Gregorian, wrote of the Jewish Division: "Today, with over a quarter of a million items, the division is one of the world's most important scholarly resources on Jewish life and history as well as one of the nation's broadest collections of historical,

literary, and classic Hebrew texts. A special characteristic of the division is the context in which it exists, as a part of the great research collection of The New York Public Library."[19]

We can continue that story to the present, a quarter of a century on, as the collection has added even more strengths to its holdings. Today The New York Public Library's Dorot Jewish Division contains a comprehensive and balanced chronicle of the religious and secular history of the Jewish people in over 300,000 books, microforms, manuscripts, newspapers, periodicals, and ephemera from all over the world. Primary source materials are especially rich in the following areas: Jews in the United States, especially in New York in the age of heavy immigration; Yiddish theater; Jews in the land of Israel through 1948; Jews in early modern Europe, especially Jewish-Gentile relations; Christian Hebraism; anti-Semitism; and world Jewish newspapers and periodicals of the nineteenth and twentieth centuries. One of the most important points, as Gregorian suggested, is its place as perhaps the greatest public collection of Judaica and Hebraica in the world, open to researchers who do not have academic or other institutional affiliations. As this volume demonstrates, its collections, rich in primary sources, thoroughly represent Jews in America from the earliest period to the present day.

Notes

1. Phyllis Dain, *The New York Public Library: A History of Its Founding and Early Years* (New York: The New York Public Library, Astor, Lenox and Tilden Foundations, 1972), 118.

2. Nathan Ausubel, "'Hippopotamus': Profile of a Great Custodian: The True Story of the Man Who Built Up the Jewish Room of The New York Public Library," *Morgn frayhayt / Morning Freiheit*, October 28, 1944 ("Freedom" magazine section), 4, 6. See http://legacy.www.nypl.org/research/chss/jws/freidus.html (accessed December 21, 2011).

3. Harry M. Lydenberg, "Freidus the Bookman," in *Studies in Jewish Bibliography and Related Subjects: In Memory of Abraham Solomon Freidus (1867–1923), Late Chief of the Jewish Division, New York Public Library* (New York: The Alexander Kohut Memorial Foundation, 1929), xlix.

4. Jenna Weissman Joselit, "Reading, Writing, and a Library Card: New York Jews and The New York Public Library," *Biblion* 5:1 (Fall 1996): 113.

5. Joshua Bloch, "The Classification of Jewish Literature in The New York Public Library," in *Studies in Jewish Bibliography and Related Subjects*, lii. The Freidus classification scheme was recently discussed by Vanessa Freedman, "The Maskil, the Kabbalist and the Political Scientist: Judaica Classification Schemes in Their Historical Context," paper given at the 46th Annual Convention of the Association of Jewish Libraries, June 19–22, 2011, Montreal.

6. Joselit, "Reading, Writing, and a Library Card," 109.

7. *Studies in Jewish Bibliography and Related Subjects*, vii.

8. Joselit, "Reading, Writing, and a Library Card," 113.

9. Abraham Berger, quoted in Anita Libman Lebeson, "Joshua Bloch ל״ז: An Appreciation," in *The Joshua Bloch Memorial Volume: Studies in Booklore and History*, ed. Abraham Berger et al. (New York: The New York Public Library, 1960), x.

10. Dora Steinglass, "A Bibliography of the Writings of Joshua Bloch," in *The Joshua Bloch Memorial Volume*, 180.

11. Joshua Bloch, "American Jewish Literature: A Tercentenary Review," *Jewish Book Annual* 12 (5715 / 1954): 17–28. The article's title is ambiguous; in fact it concerns intellectual and scholarly works, not belles-lettres.

12. Lebeson, "Joshua Bloch ל״ז," xvii.

13. Joshua Bloch, *The People and the Book: The Background of Three Hundred Years of Jewish Life in America* (New York: The New York Public Library, 1954). The exhibition was sponsored by the Louis M. Rabinowitz Foundation, a New York-based charity that supported Jewish cultural efforts.

14. Bloch, *The People and the Book*, 18.

15. Lebeson, "Joshua Bloch ל״ז," xv.

16. Dain, *The New York Public Library*, 115.

17. Ibid., 118.

18. For a history and guide to the Slavic and Baltic collections, see Robert H. Davis, Jr., *Slavic and Baltic Library Resources at The New York Public Library: A First*

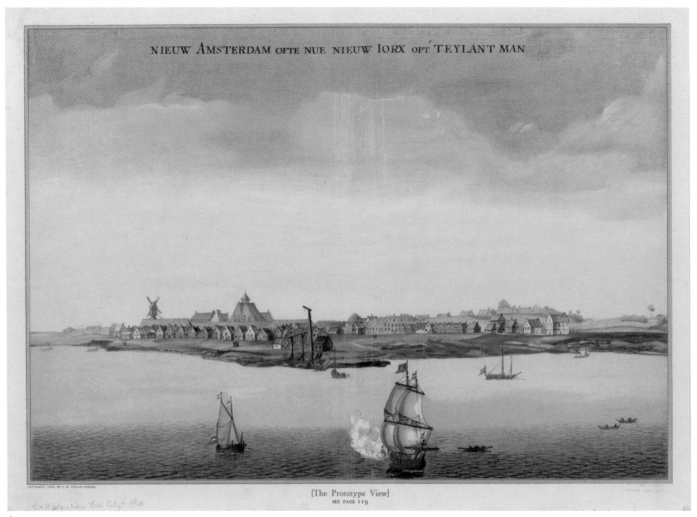

NIEUW AMSTERDAM ofte nue nieuw IORX opt' TEYLANT MAN

[The Prototype View]
SEE PAGE 119

fig. 30

History and Practical Guide (New York: The New York Public Library; Los Angeles: Chas. Schlacks, Jr., 1994).

19. Vartan Gregorian, "Foreword," in *A Sign and a Witness: 2,000 Years of Hebrew Books and Illuminated Manuscripts*, ed. Leonard Singer Gold (New York: The New York Public Library and Oxford University Press, 1988), xi.

fig. 30
"Nieuw Amsterdam ofte nue Nieuw Iorx opt' t.Eylant Man" (New Amsterdam now New York on the Island of Manhattan), from vol. 1 of I. N. Phelps Stokes, *The Iconography of Manhattan Island, 1498–1909* (New York: Robert H. Dodd, 1915–28). This "Prototype View" is a reproduction of a watercolor (ca. 1665) depicting New Amsterdam in ca. 1650–53; the original watercolor held by the Royal Archives, The Hague

Further Reading

Books

Chametzky, Jules, et al., eds. *Jewish American Literature: A Norton Anthology*. New York: Norton, 2001.

Diner, Hasia R. *The Jews of the United States, 1654 to 2000*. Berkeley and London: University of California Press, 2006.

Faber, Eli. *A Time for Planting: The First Migration, 1654–1820*. Baltimore: Johns Hopkins University Press, 1992.

Gold, Leonard Singer, ed. *A Sign and a Witness: 2,000 Years of Hebrew Books and Illuminated Manuscripts*. New York: The New York Public Library; New York and Oxford [England]: Oxford University Press, 1988.

Kagan, Richard L., and Philip D. Morgan, eds. *Atlantic Diasporas: Jews, Conversos and Crypto-Jews in the Age of Mercantilism, 1500–1800*. Baltimore: Johns Hopkins University Press, 2009.

Kaplan, Dana Evan, ed. *The Cambridge Companion to American Judaism*. Cambridge [England] and New York: Cambridge University Press, 2005.

Korn, Bertram Wallace. *American Jewry and the Civil War*. Philadelphia: Jewish Publication Society, 2001.

Marcus, Jacob Rader. *The American Jew, 1585–1900: A History*. Brooklyn, N.Y.: Carlson, 1995.

Newhouse, Alana, ed., and Chana Pollack, archivist. *A Living Lens: Photographs of Jewish Life from the Pages of the "Forward"*. New York: Forward Books; W. W. Norton & Co., 2007.

Princeton University, et al. *The Leonard L. Milberg Collection of Jewish American Writers*. 2 vols. Princeton, N.J.: Princeton University Library, 2001.

Raphael, Marc Lee, ed. *The Columbia History of Jews and Judaism in America*. New York: Columbia University Press, 2008.

Rochlin, Harriet, and Fred Rochlin. *Pioneer Jews: A New Life in the Far West*. Boston, Mass.: Houghton Mifflin, 1984.

Sarna, Jonathan D. *American Judaism: A History*. New Haven: Yale University Press, 2004.

Schloff, Linda Mack. *And Prairie Dogs Weren't Kosher: Jewish Women in the Upper Midwest since 1855*. St. Paul: Minnesota Historical Society Press, 1996.

Wenger, Beth S.. *The Jewish Americans: Three Centuries of Jewish Voices in America*. New York: Doubleday, 2007.

Periodicals

American Jewish Historical Quarterly

American Jewish History

Publications, American Jewish Historical Society

Western States Jewish History

Websites

American Jewish Historical Society
www.ajhs.org

American Jewish Archives
www.americanjewisharchives.org

National Museum of American Jewish History
www.nmajh.org

Databases (Subscription)

Jewish Life in America, c1654–1954: Sources from the American Jewish Historical Society, New York
www.jewishlife.amdigital.co.uk

Acknowledgments

Special thanks to Ann Thornton, Andrew W. Mellon
Director of The New York Public Libraries, and Cantor
Lori Corrsin of Temple Emanu-El, New York.

The authors would also like to acknowledge their
colleagues at The New York Public Library, D Giles
Limited, and beyond: Misha Anikst, Pat Barylski, Anne-
Marie Belinfante, Peter Bengston, Barbara Bergeron,
Jeanne Bornstein, Cathy Carr, Angela Carreno, Mary
Christian, Kathie Coblentz, Allison Giles, Dan Giles,
Pamela Graham, Elizabeth Hays, Denise Hibay, Rebecca
Hohmann, Rebecca Holte, Michael Inman, Matt
Knutzen, Thomas Lannon, Tom Lisanti, Sarah
McLaughlin, Abby Meisterman, Jessica Pigza, Susan
Rabbiner, Peter Riesett, David Rose, Roberta Saltzman,
Stephan Saks, Jonathan D. Sarna, Saskia Scheffer,
Katharina Seifert, Eric Shows, Victoria Steele, Anne
Skillion, and Eleanor Yadin.

Your help and advice proved invaluable throughout the
course of this project. All of you, not least the team at
Giles, went the extra mile.

Illustration Credits

All materials reproduced in *Jews in America: From New Amsterdam to the Yiddish Stage* are from the collections of The New York Public Library, Astor, Lenox and Tilden Foundations. Library collections represented in the volume are listed below. Image credits give page number, collection, and Digital ID number.

- Dorot Jewish Division (JWS)
- General Research Division (GRD)
- Manuscripts and Archives Division (MSS)
- Lionel Pincus and Princess Firyal Map Division (MAP)
- Mid-Manhattan Picture Collection (MMPC)
- Irma and Paul Milstein Division of United States History, Local History and Genealogy (LGH)
- Music Division (MUS)
- Photography Collection, The Miriam and Ira D. Wallach Division of Art, Prints and Photographs (PHG)
- Print Collection, The Miriam and Ira D. Wallach Division of Art, Prints and Photographs (PRN)
- Rare Book Division (RBK)
- Billy Rose Theatre Division (THE)

Front cover, RBK, 1804221, (standing figure)
Front cover, MMPC, 800039 (view)
Frontispiece, JWS, 2051369
6, JWS, 2051385
16, RBK, ps_rbk_cd24_371
19, 21, RBK, 1820056
22, RBK, psnypl_rbk_799
23, JWS, 2051356
24, RBK, ps_rbk_423
25, RBK, psnypl_map_248
26, RBK, ps_rbk_cd23_354
27, RBK, ps_rbk_438
28, JWS, 2051360
30, MAP, 1505029
34, JWS, 2051357
35, JWS, 2051358
36, RBK, ps_rbk_505
37, GRD, 1111964
38, MAP, 1619055
39 (above), RBK, ps_rbk_444
39 (below), RBK, ps_rbk_443
40, MAP, 1505069
41, RBK, ps_rbk_440
42–43, MAP, 1505029
45 (left), JWS, 2051361
45 (right), JWS, 2051362
46 (left), JWS, 2051364
46 (right), JWS, 2051366
49 (left), RBK, 2051368
49 (right), RBK, ps_rbk_485
51, JWS, 2051369
54, PRN, 424441
57, PRN, ps_prn_640
59 (left), MSS, ps_mss_542
59 (right), MSS, ps_mss_543
60, MSS, ps_mss_540
61, PRN, 54741
63 (left), MSS, ps_mss_538
63 (right), MSS, ps_mss_539
64–65, PRN, 54670
66–67, MAP, psnypl_map_301
68, PRN, 424441
69, PRN, 54910
70–71, RBK, 1804221
72, RBK, ps_rbk_511
76, RBK, ps_rbk_cd23_348
77 (left), RBK, 2051379
77 (right), RBK, 2051380
79 (left), RBK, 2051382
79 (right), RBK, 2051383
81 (left), RBK, ps_rbk_508
81 (right), PRN, ps_prn_cd35_510
83, RBK, ps_rbk_cd23_346
84, RBK, ps_rbk_cd23_349
85, PRN, 1808316
86, MAP, 2051372

87, RBK, ps_rbk_428
88, PRN, ps_prn_642
89, RBK, ps_rbk_531
90 (above), RBK, ps_rbk_511
90 (below), PRN, EM3358
92, RBK, 2051391
95 (left), JWS, 2051385
95 (right), JWS, 2051384
97 (left), RBK, 2051392
97 (right), JWS, 2051386
98–99, RBK, 2051370
101, RBK, ps_rbk_416
102, PRN, 424889
103, JWS, 2051373
104, RBK, ps_rbk_474
106, RBK, ps_rbk_471
109 (left), RBK, ps_rbk_393
109 (right), RBK, 2051391
110, JWS, ps_jwd_162
111, MMPC, 823818
112, PRN, 55101
116, PHG, 116960
117 (left), JWS, ps_jwd_167
117 (right), JWS, 2051434
118, PHG, 437536
120, JWS, 2051443
121, PRN, 55101
122, JWS, ps_jwd_172
123 (left), LHG, 711538f

123 (right), PRN, 1559503
124, JWS, 1945376
125, PHG, 97342
126, MUS, 2051400
129, JWS, 2051375
130 (left), PRN, 1247547
130 (right), PRN, ps_prn_cd40_581
134, JWS, 2051432
136, JWS, 1268386
139, JWS, 2051374
141, JWS, 2051452
142 (left), THE, 1689996
142 (right), JWS, 1690366
143, JWS, 2051377
144, THE, TH-16553
146, JWS, 2051354
148, PRN, 2054992
149, JWS, 2051376
Back cover, MMPC, 837003

To learn more about most of the images featured in this volume, or to buy prints (framed or unframed of them), visit the Library's Digital Gallery at digitalgallery.nypl.org, and search for the image using its Digital ID number. The Digital Gallery contains more than 800,000 high-quality images, available free for download for personal or study purposes.

www.nypl.org
www.digitalgallery.nypl.org
www.nypl.org/ask-nypl

Index